Better Homes and Gardens®
A Cross-Stitch CHRISTMAS™

Gifts to Cherish

BETTER HOMES AND GARDENS®
Des Moines, Iowa

BETTER HOMES AND GARDENS® BOOKS
An Imprint of Meredith® Books

*A CROSS-STITCH CHRISTMAS*TM
Editor: Carol Field Dahlstrom
Associate Editor: Colleen Johnson
Administrative Assistant: Peggy Daugherty
Contributing Editors: Barbara Hickey and Susan Banker
Contributing Designer: Ernie Shelton
Technical Illustrator: Chris Neubauer Graphics
Production Manager: Douglas Johnston

Editor-in-Chief, Book Group: James D. Blume
Director, New Product Development: Ray Wolf
Managing Editor: Christopher Cavanaugh

Meredith Publishing Group
President, Publishing Group: Christopher Little
Vice President and Publishing Director: John P. Loughlin

Meredith Corporation
Chairman of the Board and Chief Executive Officer: Jack D. Rehm
President and Chief Operating Officer: William T. Kerr

Chairman of the Executive Committee: E.T. Meredith III

All of us at Better Homes and Gardens® Books are dedicated to providing you with the information and ideas you need to create beautiful and useful projects. We guarantee your satisfaction with this book for as long as you own it. We welcome your questions, comments, or suggestions. Please write to us at: Cross Stitch & Needlework, Better Homes and Gardens® Books, 1912 Grand Avenue-GA308, Des Moines, IA 50309-3379.

If you would like to order additional copies of any of our books, call 1-800-678-2803 or check with your local bookstore.

Cover: Photograph by Hopkins Associates

Our "Mark of Excellence" craft seal assures you that every project in this publication has been constructed and checked under the direction of the crafts experts at Better Homes and Gardens® Cross Stitch & Country Crafts® magazine.

ISSN: 1081-468X
ISBN: 0-696-20037-6 (hardcover)
ISBN: 0-696-20479-7 (softcover)

The Christmas season brings so many joys—the love of family and friends, holiday celebrations, and thoughtful gift-giving. Handmade gifts, created for those very special people on your Christmas list, are truly the best gifts of all.
We hope that this book will delight you with just the right projects to stitch for the holidays and because those pieces will be created with joy and love in your heart, they will always be Gifts to Cherish.

A
Cross-Stitch
CHRISTMAS ™

HOLLY JOLLY SANTAS AND SNOWMEN

Stitch and give our jolly Santas and snowmen for friends and family. These delightful pieces are sure to become a part of their Christmas celebrations.

WONDERFUL WEARABLES

Catch the spirit of the holiday season by getting all decked out in spectacular holiday fashions you have stitched yourself.

FESTIVE HOLIDAY GREETINGS

Friends and family will be welcomed warmly into your holiday home with these festive greetings.

HOLLY JOLLY SANTAS AND SNOWMEN

*W*hat a delight to share the excitement of Christmas with special friends and family, and what better way to celebrate than to present lovingly stitched gifts made especially for them. We hope you enjoy our collection of jolly Santas and snowmen that you can stitch just in time for Christmas gift giving.

Start by wrapping your packages in style with our sparkling *Star Santa Ribbon* shown on this page. The simple motif is repeated on strips of white Aida fabric. The instructions and chart for the ribbon are on page 13.

Designer: Barbara Sestok ◆ Photographer: Scott Little

Santa On His Way

The big day is finally here and we've caught Santa and his reindeer making their Christmas deliveries. Capture the spellbinding magic of the Santa Claus legend by stitching this fanciful design for a collector friend (or yourself). The complete instructions and chart are on pages 13–15.

Designer: Barbara Sestok ◆ Photographer: Scott Little

Santa Mini-Banners

Herald the coming of the holiday season by crafting this charming trio of mini-banners. Decorated with individual Santa motifs, each banner is 5 inches long and is quick to stitch using a simple combination of cross-stitches and backstitches. These sweet designs make great last-minute gifts. Instructions and charts are on page 18.

Father Christmas Doorstop

Modeled after the Father Christmas of centuries past, our charming doorstop has all the kindly qualities of today's Jolly Old Elf. Create this elegant 16-inch fellow on 11-count Victorian red Aida cloth. Complete instructions and chart are on pages 16–18.

Designers: Banners, Alice Okon; Doorstop, Jim Williams
Photographer: Hopkins Associates

St. Nick Stockings

One look at these stockings and it's very clear—Santa's been here, leaving a trail of presents and candy-cane treats. Stitch this simple design in the blink of an eye on 7- or 8-count fabric for all the good little ones on your holiday list. The complete instructions and chart are on pages 18–20.

Designer: Alice Okon ◆ Photographer: Hopkins Associates

Snowman Ornaments and Shirts

Dressed in their Sunday best, our snowman and snowlady are certain to melt your heart. Stitched on 28-count Nordic blue Jobelan fabric, they make adorable ornaments. Worked on $8^1/_2$-count waste canvas on a shirt, the designs create a fanciful addition to a winter wardrobe. Instructions and charts begin on page 21.

Designer: Barbara Sestok
Photographer: Hopkins Associates

Happy Snowman Stocking

Carefree memories of wintry days spent outdoors are recalled in
this charming stocking. A rich navy background accentuates
the delicate colors of the design while blending filament adds a soft
sparkle to the snow. Instructions and chart begin on page 22.

Designer: Lorri Birmingham ◆ Photographer: Hopkins Associates

Snow Family Welcome

Extend a lighthearted welcome to your holiday guests by stitching this whimsical snow family scene. Mom, Dad, and their children have gathered in all their finery for this classic portrait. Any snow lover will be thrilled to receive such a loving gift. Instructions and chart for the festive family are on pages 26–27.

Designer: Jeff Julseth ◆ Photographer: Scott Little

★ STAR SANTA RIBBON

As shown on page 6, finished ribbon is 2¾ inches wide.

MATERIALS

Fabrics
5-inch-wide piece of 14-count white Aida cloth in desired length

2-inch-wide piece of white lightweight fusible interfacing in desired length

Threads
Cotton embroidery floss in colors listed in key

Gold braid as specified in key

Supplies
Needle

Embroidery hoop

INSTRUCTIONS

Tape or zigzag edges of fabric to prevent fraying. Find vertical center of chart and vertical center of fabric. Measure 1 inch from one end of the Aida strip; begin stitching there. Use three plies of floss or one strand of braid to work cross-stitches. Work French knots and backstitches using one ply of floss. Continue stitching pattern until desired length is reached. Centering design, trim Aida cloth to measure 3¾ inches wide. Trim the short ends 1 inch from stitching.

Press edges under ½ inch on all sides of the Aida cloth strip. Center interfacing on back of stitchery with interfacing over pressed edges of Aida cloth strip. Fuse following the manufacturer's instructions.

STAR SANTA RIBBON		
ANCHOR		DMC
002	⊡	000 White
403	■	310 Black
399	Ⅰ	318 Steel
011	☒	350 Coral
1005	◉	498 Christmas red
923	●	699 Christmas green
881	▬	945 Ivory
031	♡	3708 Watermelon
	◈	002HL Kreinik gold #8 braid

BACKSTITCH

403	╱	310 Black –all stitches

STRAIGHT STITCH

	╱	002HL Kreinik gold #8 braid – all stitches

FRENCH KNOT

403	●	310 Black –eyes

Stitch count: 70 high x 37 wide
Finished design sizes:
14-count fabric – 5 x 2⅝ inches
11-count fabric – 6⅜ x 3⅜ inches
18-count fabric – 3⅞ x 2 inches

STAR SANTA RIBBON

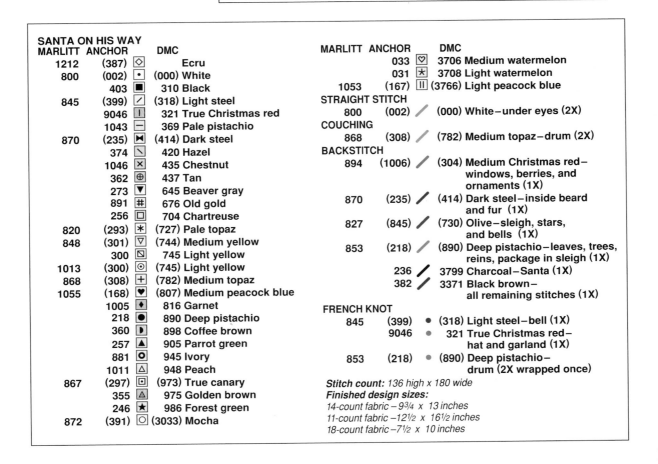

SANTA ON HIS WAY				
MARLITT	ANCHOR			DMC
1212	(387)	◇		Ecru
800	(002)	•		(000) White
	403	■		310 Black
845	(399)	╱		(318) Light steel
	9046	Ⅰ		321 True Christmas red
	1043	▬		369 Pale pistachio
870	(235)	⋈		(414) Dark steel
	374	◺		420 Hazel
	1046	☒		435 Chestnut
	362	⊕		437 Tan
	273	▼		645 Beaver gray
	891	⌗		676 Old gold
	256	▢		704 Chartreuse
820	(293)	✳		(727) Pale topaz
848	(301)	▽		(744) Medium yellow
	300	◳		745 Light yellow
1013	(300)	◉		(745) Light yellow
868	(308)	➕		(782) Medium topaz
1055	(168)	♥		(807) Medium peacock blue
	1005	◆		816 Garnet
	218	●		890 Deep pistachio
	360	▷		898 Coffee brown
	257	▲		905 Parrot green
	881	⊙		945 Ivory
	1011	△		948 Peach
867	(297)	▣		(973) True canary
	355	◬		975 Golden brown
	246	★		986 Forest green
872	(391)	◎		(3033) Mocha

	MARLITT	ANCHOR		DMC
		033	♡	3706 Medium watermelon
		031	★	3708 Light watermelon
	1053	(167)	Ⅲ	(3766) Light peacock blue

STRAIGHT STITCH

800	(002)	╱	(000) White –under eyes (2X)

COUCHING

868	(308)	╱	(782) Medium topaz–drum (2X)

BACKSTITCH

894	(1006)	╱	(304) Medium Christmas red– windows, berries, and ornaments (1X)
870	(235)	╱	(414) Dark steel–inside beard and fur (1X)
827	(845)	╱	(730) Olive–sleigh, stars, and bells (1X)
853	(218)	╱	(890) Deep pistachio–leaves, trees, reins, package in sleigh (1X)
	236	╱	3799 Charcoal–Santa (1X)
	382	╱	3371 Black brown– all remaining stitches (1X)

FRENCH KNOT

845	(399)	●	(318) Light steel–bell (1X)
	9046	●	321 True Christmas red– hat and garland (1X)
853	(218)	●	(890) Deep pistachio– drum (2X wrapped once)

Stitch count: 136 high x 180 wide
Finished design sizes:
14-count fabric – 9¾ x 13 inches
11-count fabric –12½ x 16½ inches
18-count fabric – 7½ x 10 inches

SANTA ON HIS WAY

★★★ SANTA ON HIS WAY

As shown on page 7.

MATERIALS

Fabric

15x18-inch piece of 28-count Nordic blue Jobelan fabric

Threads

Cotton embroidery floss in colors listed in key on page 13

Rayon embroidery floss in colors listed in key on page 13

Supplies

Needle

Embroidery hoop

Desired frame and mat

INSTRUCTIONS

Tape or zigzag the edges of the fabric to prevent it from fraying. Find the center of the chart and the center of the Jobelan fabric; begin stitching there.

Use three plies of cotton floss or two plies of rayon floss to work all of the cross-stitches over two threads of the Nordic blue Jobelan fabric. Work the straight stitches, couching, and the French knots as specified in the key. Work all of the back-stitches using one ply of floss. Press finished stitchery from the back. Mat and frame piece as desired.

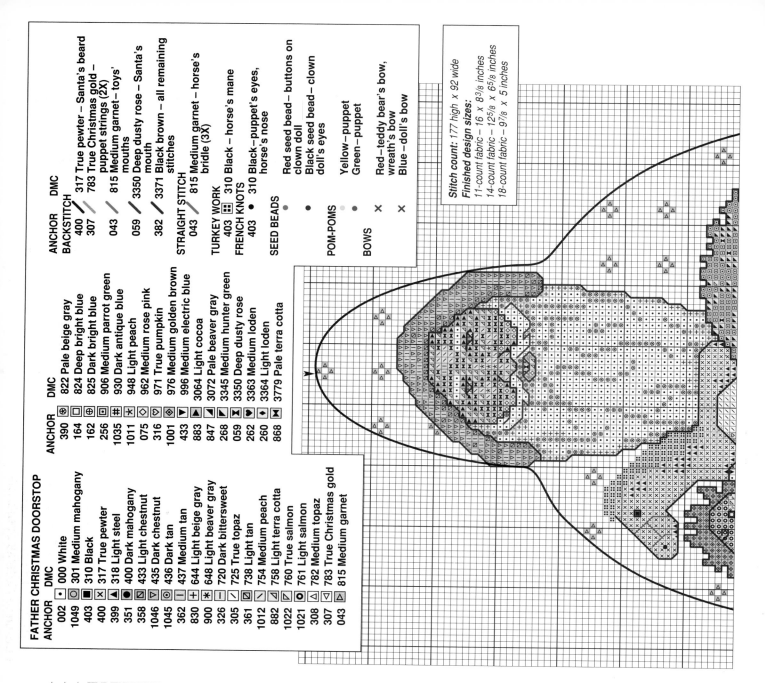

FATHER CHRISTMAS DOORSTOP

ANCHOR		DMC	
002	•	000	White
1049	⊗	301	Medium mahogany
403	■	310	Black
400	✕	317	True pewter
399	◀	318	Light steel
351	●	400	Dark mahogany
358	▷	433	Light chestnut
1046	⊙	435	Dark chestnut
1045	▶	436	Dark tan
362	▬	437	Medium tan
830	+	644	Light beige gray
900	✳	648	Light beaver gray
326			720	Dark bittersweet
305	╱	725	True topaz
361	□	738	Light tan
1012	╱	754	Medium peach
882	◩	758	Light terra cotta
1022	⊡	760	True salmon
1021	◁	761	Light salmon
308	▽	782	Medium topaz
307	▲	783	True Christmas gold
043	⊠	815	Medium garnet

ANCHOR		DMC	
390	⊗	822	Pale beige gray
164	□	824	Deep bright blue
162	⊕	825	Dark bright blue
256	▣	906	Medium parrot green
1035	#	930	Dark antique blue
1011	★	948	Light peach
075	◇	962	Medium rose pink
316	▷	971	True pumpkin
1001	⊙	976	Medium golden brown
433	▶	996	Medium electric blue
883	▲	3064	Light cocoa
847	◣	3072	Pale beaver gray
268	◤	3345	Medium hunter green
059	▶	3350	Deep dusty rose
262	◨	3363	Medium loden
260	◆	3364	Light loden
868	⊠	3779	Pale terra cotta

BACKSTITCH

ANCHOR	DMC	
400	317	True pewter – Santa's beard
307	783	True Christmas gold – puppet strings (2X)
043	815	Medium garnet – toys' mouths
059	3350	Deep dusty rose – Santa's mouth
382	3371	Black brown – all remaining stitches

STRAIGHT STITCH

043	815	Medium garnet – horse's bridle (3X)

TURKEY WORK

403	310	Black – horse's mane

FRENCH KNOTS

403	310	Black – puppet's eyes, horse's nose

SEED BEADS

Red seed bead – buttons on clown doll
Black seed bead – clown doll's eyes

POM-POMS

Yellow – puppet
Green – puppet

BOWS

Red – teddy bear's bow, wreath's bow
Blue – doll's bow

Stitch count: 177 high x 92 wide
Finished design sizes:
11-count fabric – 16 x 8 3/8 inches
14-count fabric – 12 5/8 x 6 5/8 inches
18-count fabric – 9 7/8 x 5 inches

★★★ FATHER CHRISTMAS DOORSTOP

As shown on page 8, doorstop is 16 inches tall.

MATERIALS

Fabrics

Two 20x20-inch pieces of 11-count Victorian red Aida cloth
18 x 12-inch piece of fusible fleece

Floss

Cotton embroidery floss as listed

Supplies

Needle; embroidery hoop
Erasable marker
Seed beads: 3 red and 2 black
Red sewing thread; sand
Polyester fiberfill; tracing paper
Sealing plastic sandwich bag
8½ x 4-inch piece of lightweight cardboard; 1 yard of ¼-inch-diameter white and gold cord; ⅛-inch-diameter pearl bead
Scraps of narrow red and blue satin ribbons; crafts glue
Eight ⅛-inch-diameter yellow pom-poms and seven ⅛-inch-diameter green pom-poms

INSTRUCTIONS

Tape or zigzag edges of one piece of Aida to prevent fraying. Find the center of chart and Aida cloth; begin stitching there. Use four plies to work cross-stitches. Work turkey work referring to diagram, *opposite*, using six plies. Work French knots and backstitches using two plies unless otherwise specified. Work straight stitches as specified. Attach beads using sewing thread.

Use marker to draw outline around stitched area. Fuse fleece to back of Aida. Cut out figure ¼ inch beyond line. Use stitched piece as pattern to cut back from second Aida piece.

Using marker line as guide, sew front to back, right sides together,

16

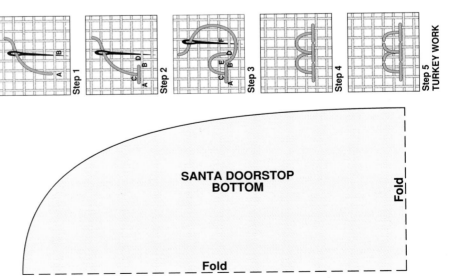

leaving the bottom open. Trim the seams and clip curves; turn right side out. Hand-stitch the cord around the figure over seam line with the ends of the cord extending beyond edges of fabric. Turn bottom raw edges under ¼ inch.

For base, fold tracing paper in half; repeat, bringing folded edges together. Matching folds, trace base pattern, *right*. Cut out; unfold. Transfer to Aida; cut out. From cardboard, cut oval ½ inch smaller than Aida. Center; glue cardboard oval to back of fabric oval. Fold raw edges to back and glue, clipping as needed.

Step 1
Step 2
Step 3
Step 4
Step 5
TURKEY WORK

SANTA DOORSTOP BOTTOM

Fold

Fold

17

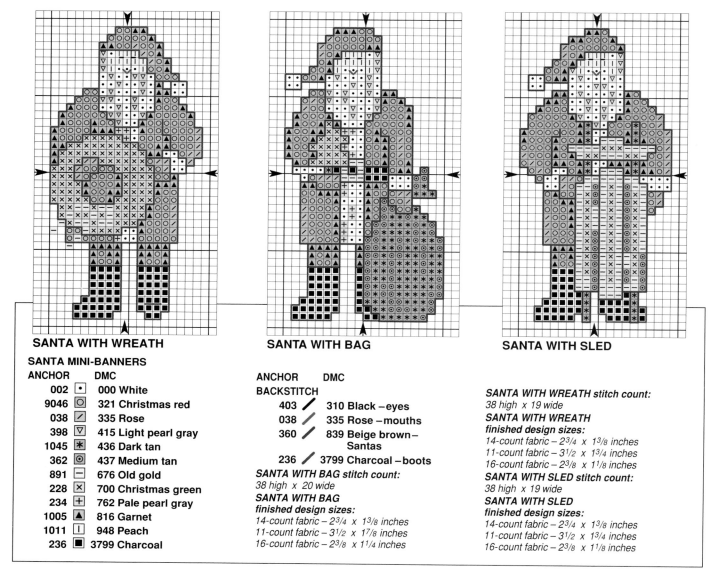

SANTA WITH WREATH **SANTA WITH BAG** **SANTA WITH SLED**

SANTA MINI-BANNERS

ANCHOR		DMC
002	•	000 White
9046	⊙	321 Christmas red
038	╱	335 Rose
398	▽	415 Light pearl gray
1045	✳	436 Dark tan
362	◉	437 Medium tan
891	−	676 Old gold
228	✕	700 Christmas green
234	+	762 Pale pearl gray
1005	▲	816 Garnet
1011	▯	948 Peach
236	◼	3799 Charcoal

ANCHOR		DMC
BACKSTITCH		
403	╱	310 Black —eyes
038	╱	335 Rose —mouths
360	╱	839 Beige brown— Santas
236	╱	3799 Charcoal —boots

SANTA WITH BAG stitch count:
38 high x 20 wide
SANTA WITH BAG
finished design sizes:
14-count fabric – 2³⁄₄ x 1³⁄₈ inches
11-count fabric – 3¹⁄₂ x 1⁷⁄₈ inches
16-count fabric – 2³⁄₈ x 1¹⁄₄ inches

SANTA WITH WREATH stitch count:
38 high x 19 wide
SANTA WITH WREATH
finished design sizes:
14-count fabric – 2³⁄₄ x 1³⁄₈ inches
11-count fabric – 3¹⁄₂ x 1³⁄₄ inches
16-count fabric – 2³⁄₈ x 1¹⁄₈ inches
SANTA WITH SLED stitch count:
38 high x 19 wide
SANTA WITH SLED
finished design sizes:
14-count fabric – 2³⁄₄ x 1³⁄₈ inches
11-count fabric – 3¹⁄₂ x 1³⁄₄ inches
16-count fabric – 2³⁄₈ x 1¹⁄₈ inches

Let glue dry. Stuff figure with fiberfill, leaving bottom 4 inches unstuffed. Fill sandwich bag with sand; seal. Insert bag into bottom of figure. Add fiberfill around bag until figure is firm. Hand-stitch base to bottom edge of figure. Tie ribbons into bows; tack to wreath and doll. Sew pearl bead to center of wreath bow. Glue pom-poms to puppet.

★ SANTA MINI-BANNERS

As shown on page 8, banners are 5 inches long.

MATERIALS *for each mini-banner*
Fabric
6-inch piece of 2³⁄₄-inch-wide 28-count white linen banding (red or green edging)

Floss
Cotton embroidery floss as listed
Supplies
Needle; embroidery hoop
Paintbrush; red paint
3⁵⁄₈-inch piece of ¹⁄₈-inch-diameter wooden dowel
Two ³⁄₈-inch-diameter wood beads
9 inches of 3-millimeter red twisted cord; crafts glue

INSTRUCTIONS
Topstitch ³⁄₄ inch from cut end on each end of banding. Find vertical center of chart and measure 1⁵⁄₈ inch from one end of banding; begin stitching top row of Santa's hat there. Use two plies to work cross-stitches over two threads. Work backstitches using one ply of floss. Press fabric under ¹⁄₄ inch on top edge; press

under ¹⁄₂ inch from folded edge. Stitch to form the casing.

Paint dowel and beads. Insert dowel into casing; glue beads on dowel ends. Tie ends of twisted cord to dowel, leaving 1-inch tails. Remove threads between cut edge and topstitching to make fringe. Tie red cord around ends of dowel.

ST. NICK STOCKINGS

As shown on page 9, finished stockings are 16 inches tall.
★★ KLOSTERN SANTA STOCKING
MATERIALS
Fabrics
19x15-inch piece of 7-count ivory Klostern fabric
³⁄₈ yard of fusible fleece

1⅝ yards of 45-inch-wide
red-and-green plaid taffeta fabric

Floss

Cotton embroidery floss in colors
listed in key on page 20

Supplies

Needle; embroidery hoop; graph
paper; pencil; erasable marker
1⅛ yards of ¼-inch-diameter cording
1⅝ yards of ⅛-inch-diameter red
cord trim
1¼ yards of 2-inch-wide red wire-
edged ribbon
30-millimeter gold jingle bell
Two 3-inch-long tassels on 12-inch
cord

INSTRUCTIONS

Chart name, separating letters
with one square. Tape or zigzag the
edges of fabric to prevent fraying.
Find the center of chart and the center of fabric; begin stitching there.
Use six plies of floss to work all the
cross-stitches. Work straight stitches
and backstitches using two plies.

Use marker to draw stocking outline around stitched area as indicated on chart. Fuse fleece to the back
of stitched fabric. Cut out the stocking ¼ inch beyond marker line.
Using the stocking as a pattern, cut
one back and two lining pieces from
the plaid fabric. Also cut a 2x40-inch
bias piping strip, a 41x4¼-inch bias
ruffle strip, and a 2½x4½-inch hanging strip.

Center cording lengthwise on
wrong side of piping strip. Fold fabric
around cording, raw edges together.
Use zipper foot to sew through both
layers ⅜ inch from the raw edges.

Baste piping around the sides and
the foot of stocking with raw edges
even, ½ inch from the raw edges.
Sew front to back, right sides together, along basting lines. Leave the top
edge open and turn. Hand sew the
red trim to the stocking between the
piping and the stocking.

Press long edges of hanging strip
under ¼ inch. Fold strip in half
lengthwise and topstitch. Fold this in
half to form a loop. Tack loop inside
the top right edge of the stocking.

Sew the short ends of ruffle strip
together to form a continuous circle.
Fold this in half lengthwise and

press. Sew a gathering thread
through both layers of the ruffle
¼ inch from the raw edges. Pull the
threads to fit the perimeter of the
stocking. Sew ruffle to the stocking
along the piping lines.

Sew lining pieces with right sides
together, leaving top open and an
opening at bottom of foot; do not
turn. Slip stocking inside lining. Stitch
stocking to lining at top edges with
right sides together; turn. Slip-stitch
opening closed. Tuck lining into
stocking; press carefully. Hand sew
red trim around top of the stocking.

Sew jingle bell to the center of the
tassel cord. Make a 7-loop bow with
the red ribbon. Tack tassels, bow,
and jingle bell to the top right corner
of the stocking. Fold cord 2 inches
from bell and tack to stocking.

★★ HEATHERFIELD
SANTA STOCKING

MATERIALS

Fabrics

19x15-inch piece of 8-count navy
Heatherfield fabric
⅜ yard each of fusible fleece and
black lightweight fusible interfacing
1⅜ yard of 45-inch-wide red-and-
green plaid taffeta fabric

Floss

Cotton embroidery floss in colors
listed in key on page 20

Supplies

Needle; embroidery hoop; graph
paper; pencil; erasable marker
1 yard of ¼-inch-diameter cording
1⅓ yards of ⅛-inch-wide red cord trim
1¼ yards of 2-inch-wide red
wire-edged ribbon
30-millimeter gold jingle bell
Two 3-inch-long tassels on 12-inch
cord

INSTRUCTIONS

Chart name, separating letters
with one square. Tape or zigzag
edges of fabric to prevent fraying.
Find center of chart and of fabric;
begin stitching there. Use four plies
of floss to work all the cross-stitches.
Work straight stitches and backstitches using two plies of floss.

Use marker to draw stocking outline around stitched area. Fuse the
interfacing to back of the stitchery

following the manufacturer's instructions. Fuse fleece to the back of the
interfacing. Cut out the stocking
¼ inch beyond marker line. Using
the stocking as a pattern, cut one
back and two lining pieces from the
plaid fabric. Also cut a 2¼x4½-inch
hanging strip, a 1½x34-inch bias
piping strip, and a 5¼x40-inch bias
ruffle strip from the taffeta fabric. All
the measurements include a ¼-inch
seam allowance.

Center cording lengthwise on
wrong side of piping strip. Fold fabric
around cording, raw edges together.
Use zipper foot to sew through both
layers ⅜ inch from the raw edges.

Baste the piping around the sides
and the foot of the stocking with raw
edges even, ½ inch from the raw
edges. Sew the front to the back,
right sides together, along basting
lines, leaving the top edge open;
turn. Hand-sew the red cord trim to
the stocking between the piping and
the stocking.

Press the long edges of the
hanging strip under ¼ inch. Fold the
strip in half lengthwise; topstitch.
Fold in half to form a loop and tack
the loop inside the top right edge of
the stocking.

Sew the short ends of the ruffle
strip together to form a continuous
circle. Fold in half lengthwise and
press. Sew a gathering thread
through both layers of the ruffle
¼ inch from the raw edges. Pull the
threads to fit the perimeter of the
stocking. Sew the ruffle to the stocking along the piping lines.

Sew lining pieces with right sides
together, leaving top open and an
opening at bottom of foot; do not
turn. Slip stocking inside the lining.
Stitch stocking to lining at top edges
with right sides together; turn. Slip-
stitch opening closed. Tuck lining
into stocking; press carefully. Hand
sew the red trim around the top of
the stocking.

Sew the jingle bell to the center of
the tassel cord. Make a 7-loop bow
with the red ribbon. Tack the tassels,
bow, and jingle bell to the top right
corner of the stocking. Fold the cord
2 inches from the bell and tack to
the stocking.

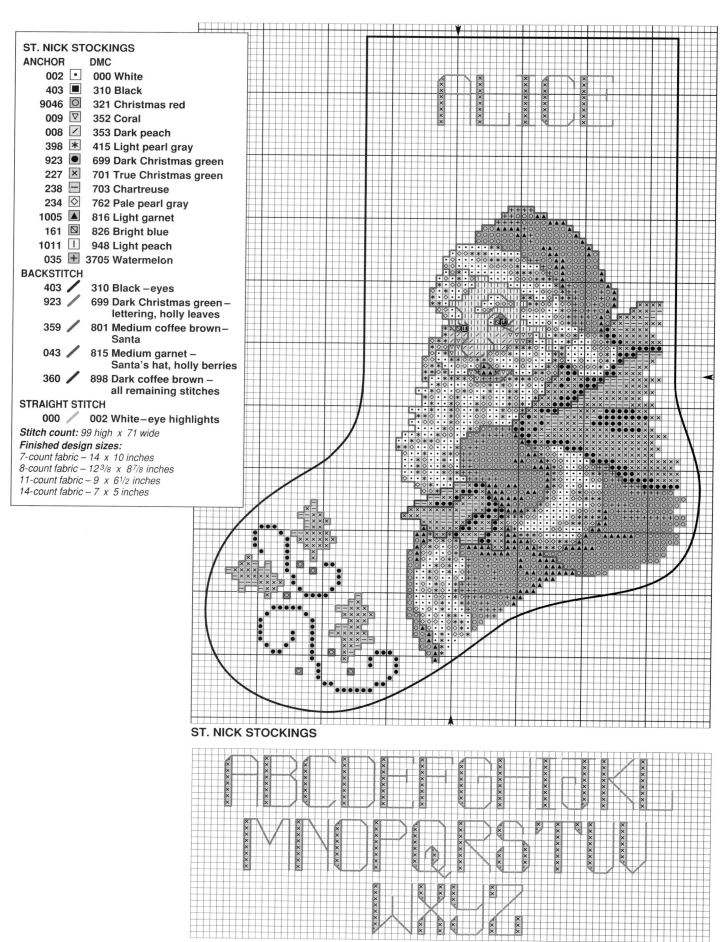

ST. NICK STOCKINGS

ANCHOR		DMC
002	•	000 White
403	■	310 Black
9046	◎	321 Christmas red
009	▽	352 Coral
008	╱	353 Dark peach
398	✳	415 Light pearl gray
923	●	699 Dark Christmas green
227	⊠	701 True Christmas green
238	—	703 Chartreuse
234	◇	762 Pale pearl gray
1005	▲	816 Light garnet
161	⊡	826 Bright blue
1011	⏐	948 Light peach
035	⊞	3705 Watermelon

BACKSTITCH

403	╱	310 Black –eyes
923	╱	699 Dark Christmas green – lettering, holly leaves
359	╱	801 Medium coffee brown – Santa
043	╱	815 Medium garnet – Santa's hat, holly berries
360	╱	898 Dark coffee brown – all remaining stitches

STRAIGHT STITCH

000	╱	002 White–eye highlights

Stitch count: 99 high x 71 wide
Finished design sizes:
7-count fabric – 14 x 10 inches
8-count fabric – 12³/₈ x 8⁷/₈ inches
11-count fabric – 9 x 6¹/₂ inches
14-count fabric – 7 x 5 inches

ST. NICK STOCKINGS

ST. NICK STOCKINGS ALPHABET

SNOWMAN AND SNOWLADY ORNAMENTS

As shown on page 10, snowman is 4 inches tall and the snowlady is 5¾ inches tall.

★★★ SNOWLADY ORNAMENT
MATERIALS
Fabrics

6x6-inch piece of 28-count Nordic blue Jobelan fabric

6x6-inch piece of blue polka-dot fabric

5x6-inch piece of white felt

Floss

Cotton embroidery floss in colors listed in key on page 22

Supplies

Needle; embroidery hoop

Erasable fabric marker; tracing paper

5x6-inch piece of self-stick mounting board with foam

6x6-inch paper-backed fusible adhesive

17-inch piece of ⅛-inch-diameter red-and-white striped cord

12-inch piece of ⅛-inch-wide flat silver braid; two 4-inch pieces of ⅛-inch-wide red ribbon

6-inch piece of ⅛-inch-wide red ribbon

INSTRUCTIONS

Tape or zigzag edges of fabric to prevent fraying. Find center of chart and fabric; begin stitching there. Use three plies of floss to work the cross-stitches over two threads of fabric. Work the French knots and straight stitches as specified in key. Work the backstitches as specified in key.

Use erasable marker to draw ornament outline on Jobelan (referring to photograph, *page 10*, include heel, toe, and cuff lines); *do not* cut out. Place tracing paper over fabric and trace ornament outline. Cut out tracing paper, making a pattern. Use pattern to cut one shape from mounting board and from felt.

For heel, toe, and cuff, extend paper pattern lines ½ inch beyond outline. Fuse paper-backed adhesive to back of blue polka-dot fabric following manufacturer's instructions. Cut out pieces, remove paper backing, and fuse to stocking. Glue silver braid over edges of blue dot fabric.

Glue a second row of braid ¼ inch above first row on cuff.

Peel protective paper from mounting board. Center foam side on back of stitched design; press to stick. Fold raw edges of fabric to back; glue. Starting at top of ornament, glue red-and-white striped cord to edge, overlapping ends at back.

Glue ends of 6-inch ribbon to each corner of stocking to make a hanger. Tie 4-inch pieces of the red ribbon into bows. Glue bows to top corners of ornament. Glue felt to back of ornament.

★★★ SNOWMAN ORNAMENT
MATERIALS
Fabrics

6x6-inch piece of 28-count Nordic blue Jobelan fabric

2x4-inch piece blue polka-dot fabric

5x5-inch piece of white felt

Threads

Cotton embroidery floss and metallic silver embroidery thread as listed in key on page 22

Supplies

Needle; embroidery hoop

Erasable fabric marker; tracing paper

4x5-inch piece of self-stick mounting board with foam

2x4-inch piece paper-backed fusible adhesive

14-inch piece of ⅛-inch-diameter blue-and-white striped cord

6-inch piece of 1/16-inch-wide red ribbon

Two 5-inch pieces of 1/16-inch-wide red ribbon; ½-inch-diameter silver jingle bell; 12-inch piece of ⅛-inch-wide flat silver braid

INSTRUCTIONS

Tape or zigzag edges of fabric to prevent fraying. Find center of chart and fabric; begin stitching there. Use three plies to work cross-stitches over two threads. Work French knots, satin stitches, and straight stitches as specified. Work the backstitches as specified in key.

Use erasable marker to draw ornament outline on Jobelan (referring to photograph, *page 10*, include bell bottom lines); *do not* cut out. Place tracing paper over fabric and trace ornament outline. Cut out the

tracing-paper pattern. Use pattern to cut one shape from mounting board and one shape from felt.

For bottom of bell, extend paper pattern lines ½ inch beyond outline. Fuse paper-backed adhesive to back of blue polka-dot fabric following manufacturer's instructions. Cut out pieces, remove paper backing; fuse to stocking. Glue silver braid over raw edges of blue dot fabric. Glue silver braid over top and bottom raw edge of blue dot fabric.

Peel paper from mounting board. Center foam side on back of stitched design; press. Fold raw edges of fabric to back; glue. Starting at top of ornament, glue blue-and-white striped cord to edge, overlapping ends at back. Fold the 6-inch ribbon in half to make loop; glue ends of ribbon to top center of ornament. Join ends of remaining ribbon; tie into bow. Glue bow to top of ornament, glue felt to back of ornament, and sew jingle bell to bottom.

★★★ SNOWMAN AND SNOWLADY SHIRTS
MATERIALS *for each shirt*
Fabrics

Purchased blue or turquoise sweatshirt

9x7-inch piece of 8½-count waste canvas; 4x5-inch piece of lightweight interfacing

Floss

Cotton embroidery floss in colors listed in key on page 22

Supplies

Needle; basting thread; tweezers

INSTRUCTIONS

Wash and dry shirt. Tape edges of waste canvas. Baste to front of sweatshirt; center left to right. Place top edge of canvas at bottom of neckband. Begin stitching top of holly on snowlady's hat 4 inches from bottom of neckband and top of snowman's cap 3½ inches from bottom of neckband. Stitch figures only, omitting background.

Use four plies to work cross-stitches. Work French knots, straight stitches, satin stitches, and backstitches using two plies. Remove basting threads; trim canvas close to stitching. Wet canvas; using

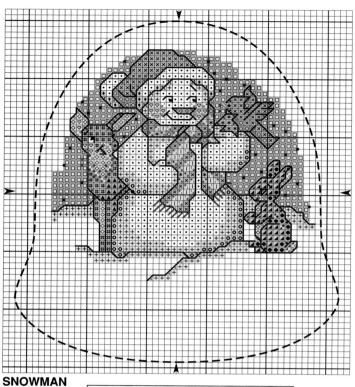

SNOWMAN

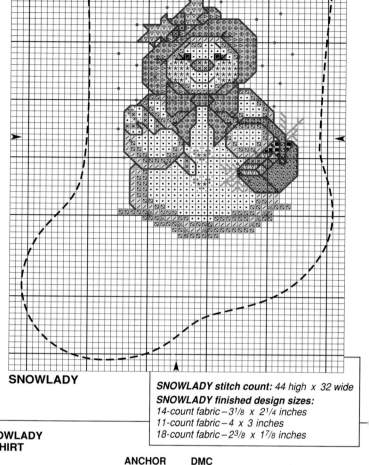

SNOWLADY

SNOWMAN stitch count: 40 high x 44 wide
SNOWMAN finished design sizes:
14-count fabric – 2⁷⁄₈ x 3¹⁄₈ inches
11-count fabric – 3⁵⁄₈ x 4 inches
18-count fabric – 2¹⁄₄ x 2³⁄₈ inches

tweezers, pull canvas threads from under cross-stitches. Fuse interfacing over stitching on inside of shirt.

★★★★ HAPPY SNOWMAN STOCKING

As shown on page 11, stocking is 20 inches tall.

MATERIALS

Fabrics

22x18-inch piece of 25-count navy Lugana fabric
19x14-inch piece fusible fleece
1 yard of white-and-navy striped fabric; ½ yard of white fabric

Threads

Cotton embroidery floss in colors listed in key on page 23
Blending filament in colors listed in key on page 23

Supplies

Needle; embroidery hoop
Graph paper; pencil; erasable marker
2 yards ¼-inch-diameter cording
6-inch piece of ¼-inch-wide white satin ribbon

22

SNOWLADY stitch count: 44 high x 32 wide
SNOWLADY finished design sizes:
14-count fabric – 3¹⁄₈ x 2¹⁄₄ inches
11-count fabric – 4 x 3 inches
18-count fabric – 2³⁄₈ x 1⁷⁄₈ inches

SNOWMAN AND SNOWLADY ORNAMENTS AND SHIRT

ANCHOR		DMC	
002	⊡	000	White
352	●	300	Deep mahogany
1049	◢	301	Medium mahogany
403	■	310	Black
399	◆	318	Steel
9046	✕	321	Christmas red
358	▲	433	Light chestnut
1046	⊞	435	Dark chestnut
228	✱	700	Medium Christmas green
226	▽	702	Light Christmas green
256	▯	704	Chartreuse
890	⊠	729	Old gold
885	◇	739	Tan
314	◉	741	Tangerine
128	⊠	775	Light baby blue
131	⊙	798	Dark Delft blue
130	+	809	True Delft blue
1005	⊘	816	Garnet
160	▢	827	Powder blue
381	★	938	Coffee brown
050	♡	957	Geranium
144	╱	3325	True baby blue
036	✳	3326	Rose
035	▷	3705	Dark watermelon
033	⊕	3706	Medium watermelon

BACKSTITCH

403	╱	310	Black –snowman, deer, rabbit, bird (1X)
9046	╱	321	Christmas red– snowlady's mouth (2X)

ANCHOR		DMC	
226	╱	702	Light Christmas green– greenery in basket (2X)
162	╱	825	Bright blue– snow (1X)
382	╱	3371	Black brown– snowlady (1X)

STRAIGHT STITCH

403	╱	310	Black –rabbit nose, snowman eyebrows, deer eyebrows (2X)
1005	╱	816	Garnet –snowman scarf (2X)

FRENCH KNOT

002	●	000	White–snowlady eyes (1X); snowflakes around snowlady (2X)
403	●	310	Black–snowman, deer, rabbit eyes (1X)
9046	●	321	Christmas red–berries in basket (2X)
228	●	700	Medium Christmas green–wreath around deer (1X)
1005	●	816	Garnet–berries in bird's beak, wreath around deer (1X)
382	●	3371	Black brown–basket handle (1X)
	●		283 DMC Light silver metallic embroidery thread– snowflakes around snowman

SATIN STITCH

314	╲	741	Tangerine–cardinal's beak (2X)

Fourteen 6½-inch pieces of ⅛-inch-wide white satin ribbon 2¾ yard of 1½-inch-wide white ribbon; 28 1-inch-wide white plastic snowflakes; crafts glue

INSTRUCTIONS

Chart name; separate letters with two squares. Tape edges of fabric to prevent fraying. Find center of chart and fabric; begin stitching there. Use three plies of floss to work cross-stitches over two threads. Work blended needle as specified. Work French knots and backstitches using one ply unless otherwise specified.

Use marker to draw outline around stitched area. Fuse fleece to back of fabric. Cut out ¼ inch beyond line. Using stocking as pattern, cut one back and two lining pieces from striped fabric. Also cut a 2¼x55-inch bias ruffle strip and a 1x45-inch bias strip for outside piping. Center cording lengthwise on wrong side of striped piping strip. Fold fabric around cording, raw edges together. Use zipper foot to sew through both layers ⅜ inch from raw edges. Cut 1x20-inch bias strip for top piping. Sew white piping in same manner.

Baste striped piping around sides and foot of stocking, raw edges even, ½ inch from raw edges. Sew front to back, right sides together, along basting lines. Leave top edge open; turn. Baste white piping around top of stocking; raw edges even. Sew short ends of ruffle strip together to form a continuous circle. Fold in half lengthwise; press. Sew gathering thread through layers of ruffle ¼ inch from raw edges. Pull threads to fit perimeter. Sew ruffle to stocking along piping lines. Fold ¼-inch ribbon in half; tack inside top right edge of stocking.

Sew lining pieces together, right sides facing, leaving top open and an opening at bottom of foot; *do not* turn. Slip stocking inside lining. Stitch stocking to lining at top edges, right sides facing; turn. Sew opening closed. Tuck lining into stocking; press. Glue two snowflakes on one end of each satin ribbon. Join opposite ribbon ends. Make 14-loop bow with white ribbon; tack snowflakes and bow to top right corner.

HAPPY SNOWMAN STOCKING

ANCHOR	DMC	
002	●	000 White
110	◆	208 Dark lavender
109	◣	209 Medium lavender
108	⌐	210 Light lavender
895	◈	223 Medium shell pink
893	○	224 Light shell pink
1049	✖	301 Medium mahogany
400	○	317 True pewter
215	✕	320 True pistachio
011	◉	350 Medium coral
010	◁	351 Light coral
009	▤	352 Pale coral
5975	◤	356 Medium terra cotta
217	●	367 Medium pistachio
214	▷	368 Light pistachio
1047	▽	402 Pale mahogany
401	⊞	413 Dark pewter
235	#	414 Steel
310	⊞	434 Medium chestnut
878	▶	501 Dark blue green
877	☒	502 Medium blue green
875	⊟	503 True blue green
868	◿	553 Medium violet
098	✚	554 Light violet
096	◁	676 Light old gold
891	╱	680 Dark old gold
901	✲	725 True topaz
305	★	

ANCHOR	DMC	
295	▷	726 Light topaz
293	□	727 Pale topaz
890	▱	729 Medium old gold
1012	—	754 Peach
882	‖	758 Light terra cotta
1022	⊕	760 True salmon
1021	△	761 Light salmon
234	▲	762 Pearl gray
136	▽	799 Medium Delft blue
144	◤	800 Pale Delft blue
359	◣	801 Coffee brown
130	⊞	809 True Delft blue
1001	⊗	976 Medium golden brown
1002	▨	977 Light golden brown
059	◙	3350 Deep dusty rose
068	◐	3687 True mauve
060	▷	3688 Medium mauve
1027	◀	3722 True shell pink
076	⊘	3731 Dark dusty rose
075	⊠	3733 Medium dusty rose
1048	⊡	3776 Light mahogany
1013	⊖	3778 True terra cotta
868	◹	3779 Pale terra cotta
236	■	3799 Charcoal
363	⊠	3827 Pale golden brown
890	◆	3829 Deep old gold

ANCHOR	DMC	
BLENDED NEEDLE		
306	✪	3820 Straw (2X) and 002 Kreinik gold blending filament (1X)
002	‖	000 White (2X) and 032 Kreinik pearl filament (1X)
128	◇	775 Light baby blue (2X) and 032 Kreinik pearl filament (1X)
144	✛	3325 True baby blue (2X) and 032 Kreinik pearl filament (1X)
1031	◺	3753 Antique blue (2X) and 032 Kreinik pearl filament (1X)
140	◉	3755 Medium baby blue (2X) and 032 Kreinik pearl filament (1X)
BACKSTITCH		
110	╱	208 Dark lavender – snowman's hat band, scarf, boy's hat, girl's hat, present
217	╱	367 Medium pistachio – holly leaves
401	╱	413 Dark pewter–top border, boy's hat trim and scarf, girl's hat trim
310	╱	434 Medium chestnut – snowman nose, boy's and girl's faces, boy's coat pocket, yellow ribbons and present, girl's shoe
878	╱	501 Dark blue green – ribbons on presents in sled

ANCHOR	DMC	
136	╱	799 Medium Delft blue – present, heart on sled, boy's and girl's eyes
1001	╱	976 Medium golden brown – girl's hair
1027	╱	3722 True shell pink –outer edge of girl's coat
059	╱	3350 Deep dusty rose – holly berries, sled, present
140	╱	3755 Medium baby blue – snowman
236	╲	3799 Charcoal –snowman's hat, eyes, mouth
306	╱	3820 Straw –name
359	╲	801 Coffee brown– all remaining stitches
BLENDED STRAIGHT STITCH		
002	╱	000 White (2X) and 032 Kreinik pearl filament (1X)– snowflakes
FRENCH KNOT		
002	●	000 White–snowflakes
359	●	801 Coffee brown–button on boy's pant cuff

Stitch count: 227 high x 154 wide
Finished design sizes:
12½-count fabric – 18 x 12⅜ inches
14-count fabric – 16 x 11 inches
18-count fabric – 12⅝ x 8½ inches

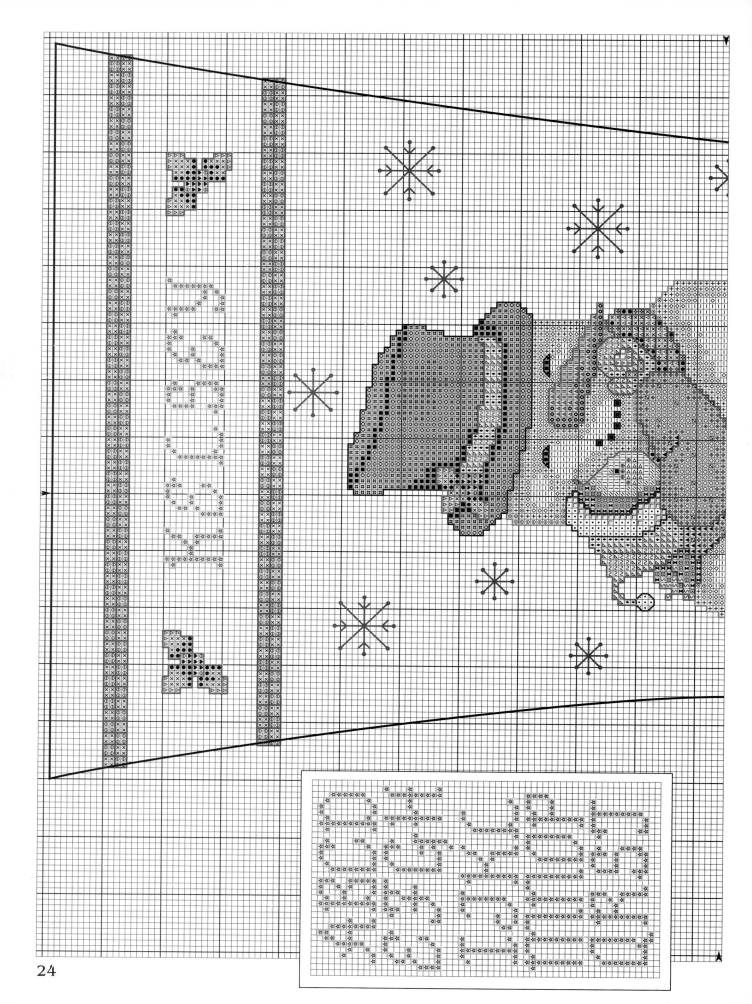

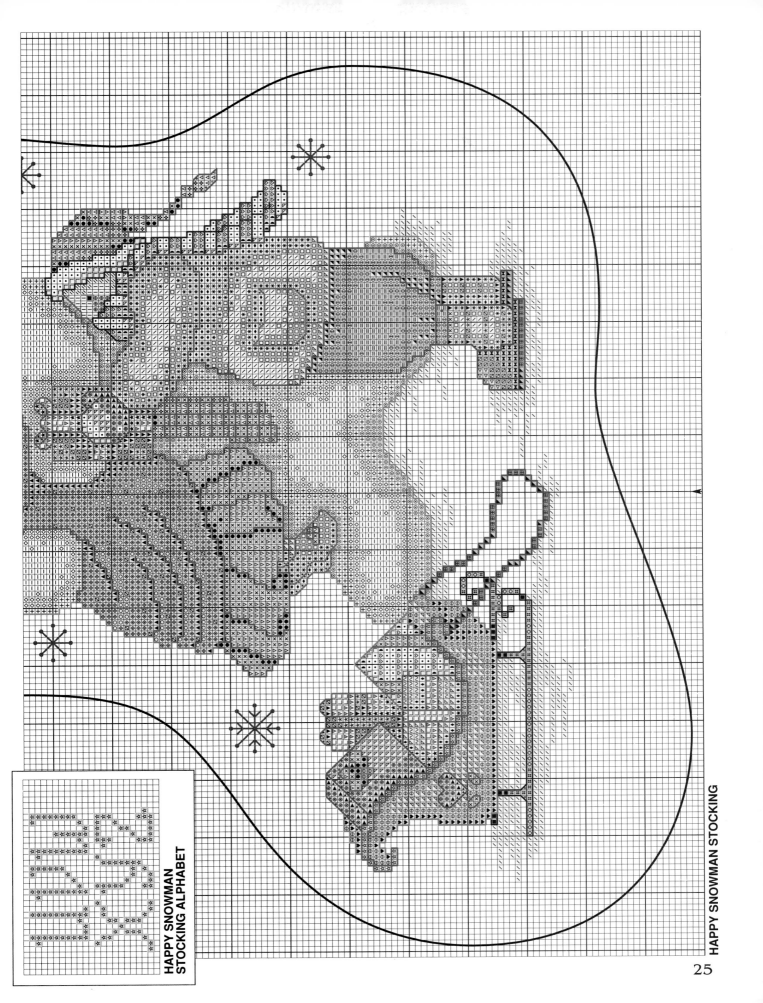

HAPPY SNOWMAN
STOCKING ALPHABET

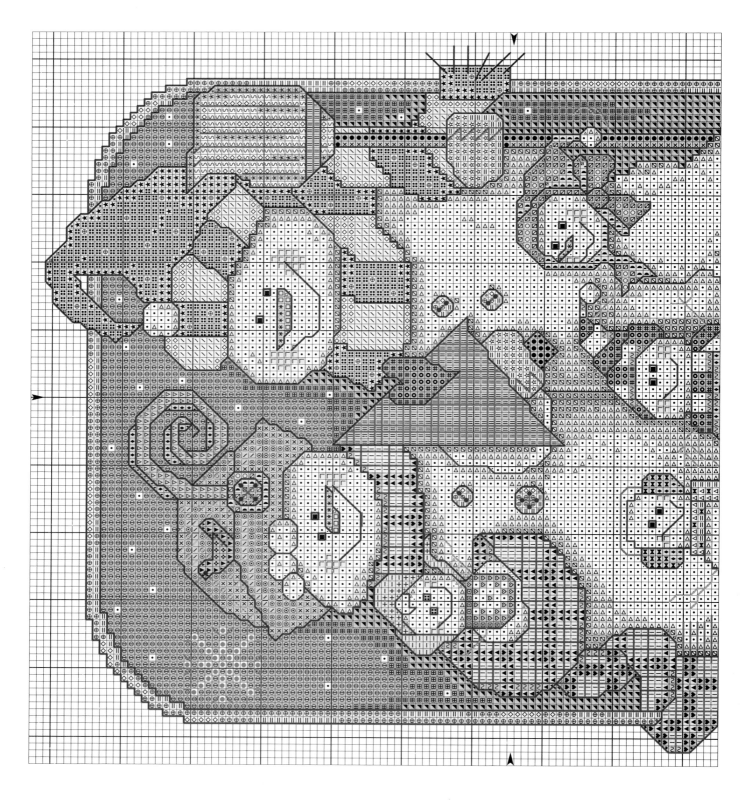

★★★★ SNOW FAMILY WELCOME

As shown on page 12.

MATERIALS

Fabric

18x13-inch piece of 28-count pewter Jubilee fabric

Floss

Cotton embroidery floss in colors listed in key on page 27

Supplies

Needle; embroidery hoop
2½-millimeter pearls
Desired frame and mat

INSTRUCTIONS

Tape or zigzag the edges of the 28-count pewter Jubilee fabric to prevent it from fraying while stitching. Find the center of the chart and the center of the fabric; begin stitching design there.

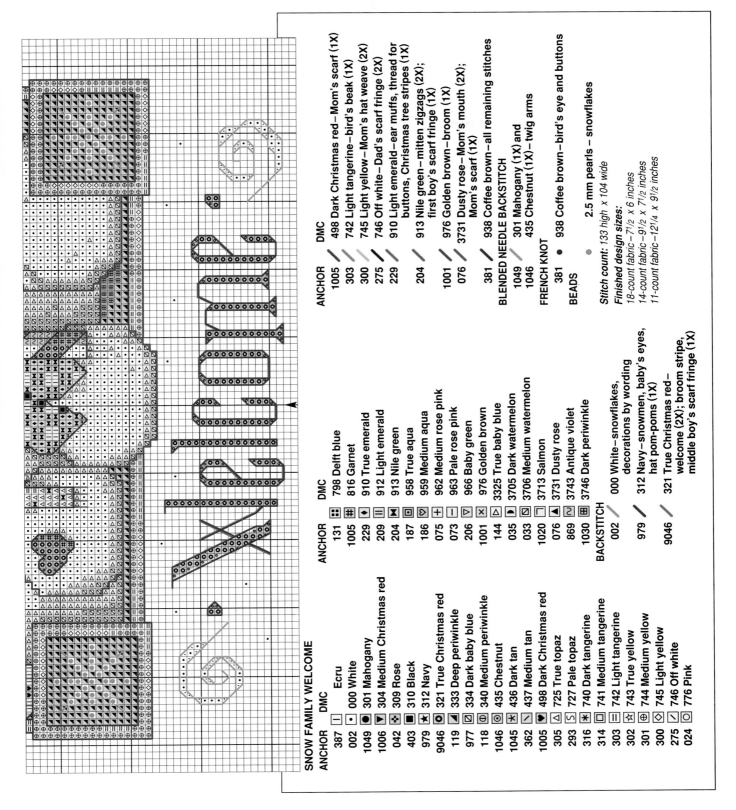

SNOW FAMILY WELCOME

ANCHOR		DMC	
387	⊟		Ecru
002	•	000	White
1049	●	301	Mahogany
1006	▶	304	Medium Christmas red
042	✚	309	Rose
403	■	310	Black
979	★	312	Navy
9046	◐	321	True Christmas red
119	◣	333	Deep periwinkle
977	◨	334	Dark baby blue
118	⊖	340	Medium periwinkle
1046	◉	435	Chestnut
1045	✳	436	Dark tan
362	◪	437	Medium tan
1005	▶	498	Dark Christmas red
305	△	725	True topaz
293	⏃	727	Pale topaz
316	◩	740	Dark tangerine
314	▣	741	Medium tangerine
303	⚌	742	Light tangerine
302	✶	743	True yellow
301	⊕	744	Medium yellow
300	◈	745	Light yellow
275	⟋	746	Off white
024	◎	776	Pink

ANCHOR		DMC	
131	⊞	798	Delft blue
1005	⌗	816	Garnet
229	◆	910	True emerald
209	⚌	912	Light emerald
204	✕	913	Nile green
187	▣	958	True aqua
186	▷	959	Medium aqua
075	✛	962	Medium rose pink
073	I	963	Pale rose pink
206	▷	966	Baby green
1001	✕	976	Golden brown
144	△	3325	True baby blue
035	◗	3705	Dark watermelon
033	◨	3706	Medium watermelon
1020	◁	3713	Salmon
076	◀	3731	Dusty rose
869	⟎	3743	Antique violet
1030	⊞	3746	Dark periwinkle

BACKSTITCH

002	╱	000	White—snowflakes, decorations by wording
979	╱	312	Navy—snowmen, baby's eyes, hat pom-poms (1X)
9046	╱	321	True Christmas red—welcome (2X); broom stripe; middle boy's scarf fringe (1X)

ANCHOR		DMC	
1005	╱	498	Dark Christmas red—Mom's scarf (1X)
303	╱	742	Light tangerine—bird's beak (1X)
300	╱	745	Light yellow—Mom's hat weave (2X)
275	╱	746	Off white—Dad's scarf fringe (2X)
229	╱	910	Light emerald—ear muffs, thread for buttons, Christmas tree stripes (1X)
204	╱	913	Nile green—mitten zigzags (2X); first boy's scarf fringe (1X)
1001	╱	976	Golden brown—broom (1X)
076	╱	3731	Dusty rose—Mom's mouth (2X); Mom's scarf (1X)
381	╱	938	Coffee brown—all remaining stitches

BLENDED NEEDLE BACKSTITCH

1049	╱	301	Mahogany (1X) and
1046		435	Chestnut (1X)—twig arms

FRENCH KNOT

381	●	938	Coffee brown—bird's eye and buttons

BEADS

●		2.5 mm pearls — snowflakes

Stitch count: 133 high x 104 wide

Finished design sizes:
18-count fabric – 7½ x 6 inches
14-count fabric – 9½ x 7½ inches
11-count fabric – 12¼ x 9½ inches

Use three plies of the cotton embroidery floss to work all of the cross-stitches over two threads of the Jubilee fabric. Work the French knots using two plies of floss. Attach the 2½-millimeter pearls using two plies of white (DMC 000) cotton embroidery floss. Work all of the backstitches using one ply of embroidery floss unless otherwise specified in the key.

Press the finished stitchery from the back. Mat and frame the piece as desired.

WONDERFUL WEARABLES

There's sure to be special people on your gift-giving list who appreciate one-of-a-kind, handmade fashions and accessories. Shop these pages to gather ideas and inspiration for items to make and give for the holidays or all year round.

To embellish your gift boxes, top them off with a band of handsome crested cardinals, shown here. After the holidays, use them as sashes, ties, or hair ribbons. Complete instructions and chart are on page 34.

Designer: Barbara Sestok ◆ Photographer: Scott Little

Poinsettia Vest

You'll steal the scene in our festive vest of stitched red poinsettias. Shimmering gold threads and paillettes lend an elegant look for formal festivities or for a perfect at-home Christmas evening. To make stitching easier, the design is cross-stitched first, then panels are stitched into the vest. Instructions and charts begin on page 34.

Designer: Ruth Schmuff
Photographer: Hopkins Associates

29

Peppermint Diamonds Jewelry

Metallic threads can yield spectacular results—and this jewelry is proof. The simple candy-cane stripes become boldly sophisticated with the addition of shining gold and crystal beads. Perforated plastic makes the jewelry lightweight. Instructions and charts begin on page 36.

Designer: Ruth Schmuff
Photographer: Hopkins Associates

Black and Gold Jewelry

This geometric pin and earring set works up so quickly, you'll want to make some for each of your holiday outfits. Because only two colors of thread are used, you can easily customize the design to match your wardrobe. Instructions and charts are on pages 38–39.

Designer: Ruth Schmuff
Photographer: Scott Little

Celestial Button Covers

Delicate seed beads transform squares of perforated plastic into
clever button covers of starry proportions. They're perfect any time
of the year. The instructions and charts are on page 40.

Designer: Ruth Schmuff ◆ Photographer: Hopkins Associates

Musical-Note Buttons

Miniature stitches strike a pleasing
chord on these petite musical-note
buttons. Worked over one thread of
linen, these tiny accessories will score
big with budding music stars and
experienced musicians alike. Instructions
and charts begin on page 39.

Designer: Linda Gordanier Jary
Photographer: Hopkins Associates

31

Skiing Cat Duplicate-Stitch Sweater

Your favorite feline fan will howl with delight over this whimsical duplicate-stitch sweater. A sprinkling of bead snowflakes adds a bit of sparkle and randomly stitched paw prints scamper up one sleeve making this design the proverbial cat's meow. Instructions and charts begin on page 40.

Designer: Jeff Julseth ◆ Photographer: Hopkins Associates

Holly and Hearts Pinafore and Vest

A crisp white pinafore with a repeat design of a holly and hearts motif cross-stitched at the hemline is the perfect topper for a holiday dress. We used a plain purchased pinafore and a pretty red dress, but you could buy or make any combination of colors and fabrics. The same design will work well across the top of a bibbed pinafore, too. For festive fellows, stitch a single holly motif on a purchased red vest. Instructions and chart are on page 41.

Designer: Virginia Soskin ◆ Photographer: Hopkins Associates

★★ CARDINAL RIBBON

As shown on page 28, ribbon is 2³⁄₄ inches wide.

MATERIALS

Fabrics

5-inch-wide piece of 14-count ivory new Gardasse fabric in desired length

2¹⁄₄-inch-wide piece of lightweight fusible interfacing in desired length

Threads

Cotton embroidery floss as listed in the key

Gold braid as specified in the key

Supplies

Needle; embroidery hoop

INSTRUCTIONS

Tape or zigzag the edges of the Gardasse fabric to prevent them from fraying. Find the vertical center of the chart and the vertical center of the fabric. Measure 1 inch from one narrow end of the fabric; begin stitching there.

Use three plies of embroidery floss or one strand of braid to work the cross-stitches. Work French knots using one ply. Work the back-stitches using one ply of embroidery floss or one strand of braid, except bird's feet. Continue stitching the pattern to the desired length.

Centering the design, trim the fabric to 3³⁄₄ inches wide. Trim the short ends of the ribbon 1 inch from the stitching.

Press the fabric edges under ¹⁄₂ inch on all sides. Pin or baste it in place. Center the interfacing on the back of the stitchery so that the interfacing goes over the pressed edges and holds them in place.

Fuse the interfacing to the back of the fabric following the manufacturer's instructions.

Note: Finished ribbons can be used as bookmarks, hairbows, sashes, and other decorative items as well as package trims.

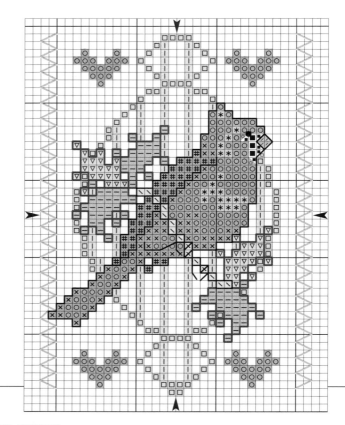

CARDINAL RIBBON

ANCHOR		DMC	
403	■	310	Black
1025	✕	347	Deep salmon
013	◉	349	Dark coral
228	⊟	700	Christmas green
256	☐	704	Chartreuse
326	◢	720	Bittersweet
890	◥	729	Old gold
203	▽	954	Nile green
033	✳	3706	Watermelon
1015	⊞	3777	Terra cotta
	⊡	002	Kreinik gold #8 braid

ANCHOR		DMC	
BACKSTITCH			
218	╱	890	Pistachio–leaves
	╱	002	Kreinik gold #8 braid–border
236	╱	3799	Charcoal–bird's feet (2X); all remaining stitches (1X)
FRENCH KNOT			
236	●	3799	Charcoal–bird's eye

Stitch count: 47 high x 34 wide
Finished design sizes:
14-count fabric – 3³⁄₈ x 2 inches
11-count fabric – 4¹⁄₄ x 3 inches
18-count fabric – 2⁵⁄₈ x 2 inches

★★★★ POINSETTIA VEST

As shown on page 29.

MATERIALS

Fabrics

55-inch-wide piece of 25-count antique white Lugana fabric in amount specified on pattern

POINSETTIA VEST–TOP

Ivory fabric for vest lining and
    backing in amount specified
    on pattern
Threads
Cotton embroidery floss in colors
    listed in key on page 37
Kreinik #8 braid in colors listed
    in key on page 37
Kreinik gold 002C cord

Supplies
Purchased vest pattern
    without pockets
Erasable fabric marker
Needle; embroidery hoop
Kreinik #4 gold paillettes
    (flat sequins)
Notions as specified on pattern
Matching sewing thread

INSTRUCTIONS
   Trace the vest fronts onto the
Lugana fabric with fabric marker,
allowing 2 inches between each of
the outlines.
   Omit pockets or pocket flaps and
buttonhole and button markings.
Serge or zigzag the fabric edges to
prevent fraying.

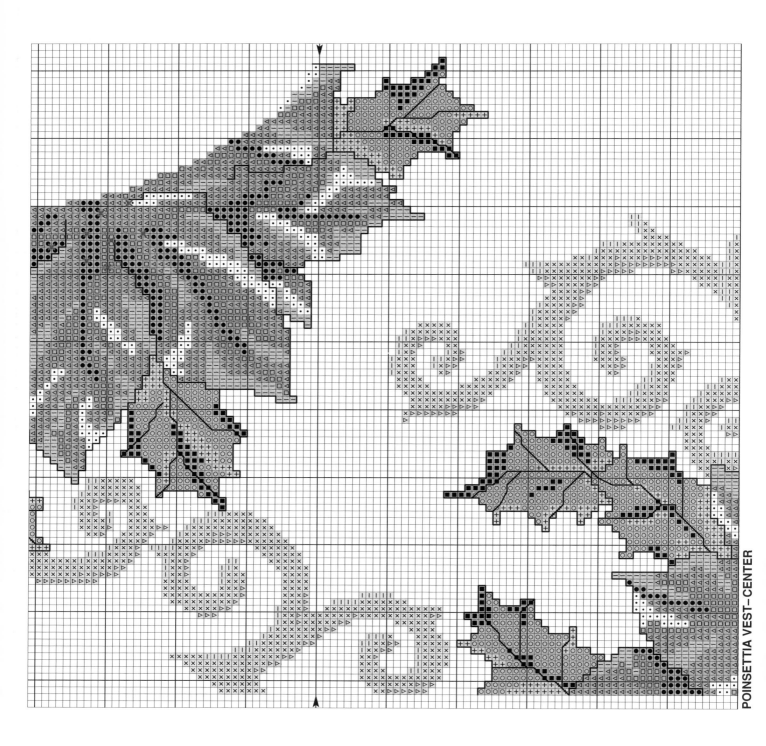

POINSETTIA VEST–CENTER

For left front (as worn), measure 1¼ inches from edges of shoulder and ¾ inch from front edge, on straight grain; begin stitching top poinsettia petal there. Use three plies of floss or one strand of braid to work cross-stitches over two threads of fabric. Work backstitches using one strand of braid. Use two strands of cord to attach paillettes or the sequins.

Work right front as directed for left front, *except*, flip chart the opposite direction. Redraw vest outlines. Cut out vest fronts, vest back, lining or facings, and back ties, if included, according to pattern. Sew vest following pattern instructions.

PEPPERMINT DIAMONDS JEWELRY

As shown on page 30, pin is 3⅜ inches long; earrings are ⅞ x ⅞ inches.

★★ PEPPERMINT DIAMONDS PIN
MATERIALS
Fabric

2 x 4-inch piece of 14-count clear perforated plastic

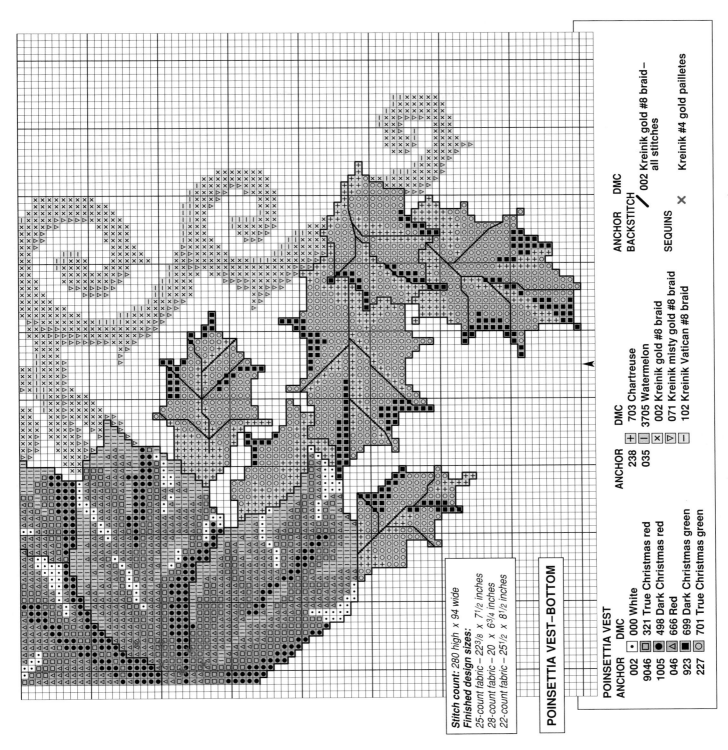

ANCHOR DMC BACKSTITCH
/ 002 Kreinik gold #8 braid– all stitches

SEQUINS
✕ Kreinik #4 gold pailletes

ANCHOR	DMC	
	703	Chartreuse
	3705	Watermelon
	002	Kreinik gold #8 braid
	071	Kreinik misty gold #8 braid
	102	Kreinik Vatican #8 braid

ANCHOR	DMC		
238	+		
035	−		
	✕		
	▷		
	I		

POINSETTIA VEST

ANCHOR	DMC		
002	•	000	White
9046	☐	321	True Christmas red
1005	●	498	Dark Christmas red
046	◁	666	Red
923	■	699	Dark Christmas green
227	○	701	True Christmas green

Stitch count: 280 high x 94 wide
Finished design sizes:
25-count fabric – 22³⁄₈ x 7¹⁄₂ inches
28-count fabric – 20 x 6³⁄₄ inches
22-count fabric – 25¹⁄₂ x 8¹⁄₂ inches

POINSETTIA VEST–BOTTOM

Threads

¹⁄₁₆-inch ribbon in colors listed in key on page 38

#16 braid in color listed in key on page 38

Supplies

Needle

42 gold seed beads

Four ¹⁄₄-inch-long clear crystal beads

Five ¹⁄₈-inch-long clear crystal beads

1 x 1-inch red bow charm

1¹⁄₂ x 4-inch piece of white felt

2-inch-long pin back

All-purpose cement

INSTRUCTIONS

Find center of the pin chart and center of the perforated plastic; begin stitching there. Use one strand of braid or ribbon to work the *half* cross-stitches. Work the padded diamond stitches, *page 38,* using one strand of ribbon. Trim the plastic one square beyond the stitches. Cut a matching felt back. Whipstitch edges using one strand of ribbon. Thread needle with sewing thread.

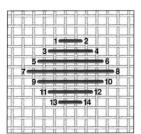
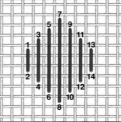
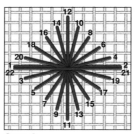

Step 1
Padded Diamond Stitch

Step 2

Step 3

PEPPERMINT DIAMONDS JEWELRY
⊠ 002 Kreinik gold 1/16" ribbon
☑ 003 Kreinik red 1/16" ribbon
• 032 Kreinik pearl #16 braid
PADDED DIAMOND STITCH
╱ 003 Kreinik red #16 braid
PIN stitch count: 11 high x 44 wide
PIN finished design size:
14-count fabric – 7/8 x 3 1/2 inches
EARRING stitch count: 11 high x 11 wide
EARRING finished design size:
14-count fabric – 7/8 x 7/8 inches

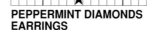

PEPPERMINT DIAMONDS EARRINGS

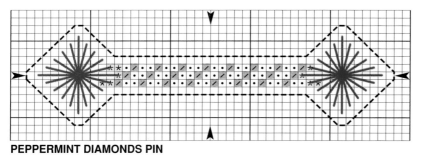

PEPPERMINT DIAMONDS PIN

Insert needle from back at 1 inch from point. Thread 5 gold beads, small crystal, 5 gold beads, large crystal, 5 gold beads, small crystal, 5 gold beads, large crystal, 5 gold beads, small crystal.

Return the needle to the back at the opposite end of the pin 1 1/4 inch from the point and secure.

Tack the bow charm to the bottom of pin on right side. On the left side, add gold bead, large crystal, gold charm. Return the thread through beads, to back; secure. Glue felt to back; glue pin back to center of back.

★ **PEPPERMINT DIAMOND EARRINGS**
MATERIALS
Fabric
Two 2x2-inch pieces 14-count perforated plastic

Threads
1/16-inch ribbon and #16 braid in colors listed in the key
Supplies
Needle; six gold seed beads
Two 1/4-inch-long clear crystal beads
Two 1x1-inch pieces white felt
Two post or clip-style earring backs
All-purpose cement

INSTRUCTIONS
Find center of earring chart and center of perforated plastic; begin stitching there. Use one strand of ribbon to work the padded diamond stitches (see the stitching diagram above). Trim the plastic one square beyond the stitched area of the design. Cut a matching felt back. Whipstitch the edges using one strand of ribbon.

Insert the needle and thread through the bottom point from the back. Thread on gold seed bead, small crystal bead, and two gold seed beads. Return the thread through the beads to earring; secure. Glue the felt to back, then glue the earring backs in place using the all-purpose cement. To make the earrings lay flat, off-set the backs slightly toward the top.

BLACK AND GOLD JEWELRY

As shown on page 30, pin is 1 3/4 x 2 1/4 inches; earrings are 1 1/4 x 7/8 inches.
★★ **BLACK AND GOLD PIN**
MATERIALS
Fabric
3x4-inch piece of 14-count clear perforated plastic
Threads
#16 braid in color listed in key
1/16-inch ribbon in colors listed in key on page 39
Supplies
Needle
One 3/8-inch-long black crystal bead
Two 1/4-inch-long black crystal beads
Three black seed beads
2 1/2x3-inch piece of white felt
1-inch-long pin back
All-purpose cement

INSTRUCTIONS
Find the center of the chart and the center of plastic; begin stitching there. Use one strand of braid to work the half cross-stitches. Use one strand of 1/16-inch ribbon to work the Rhodes stitches referring to the diagrams, *opposite*.

Trim the plastic one square beyond the stitching; cut a matching felt back. Whipstitch the edges of the plastic using one strand of the gold braid.

Insert the needle and thread through the bottom point of the pin from back. Thread on large bead, then seed bead. Return through the bead to pin; secure.

Attach a small crystal and a seed bead at each of the side points. Glue the felt to the back of the pin. Glue the pin back to the felt.

**BLACK AND GOLD
EARRINGS**

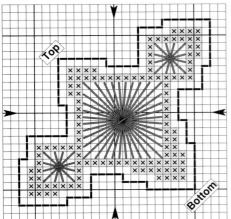

BLACK AND GOLD PIN

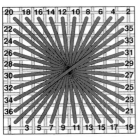

Large Rhodes Stitch

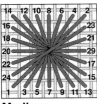

**Medium
Rhodes Stitch**

**Small
Rhodes Stitch**

BLACK AND GOLD JEWELRY
CONTINENTAL STITCH
⊠ 002HL Kreinik Aztec gold
#16 braid
RHODES STITCH
╱ 005 Kreinik black
1/16" ribbon
EARRING stitch count: 10 high x 10 wide
EARRING finished design size:
14-count fabric – 3/4 x 3/4 inches
PIN stitch count: 22 high x 22 wide
PIN finished design size:
14-count fabric – 1 5/8 x 1 5/8 inches

★ **BLACK AND
GOLD EARRINGS**
MATERIALS
Fabric
Two 2x2-inch pieces of 14-count
clear perforated plastic
Threads
#16 braid in color listed in key
1/16-inch ribbon in colors listed
in key
Supplies
Needle
Two 1/4-inch-long black
crystal beads
Three black seed beads
3x3-inch piece of white felt
Earring backs—clip style or post
style with a back
All-purpose cement

INSTRUCTIONS
Find the center of the chart and
the center of the plastic; begin stitching there. Use one strand of ribbon
to work Rhodes stitches referring to
the stitching diagrams, *left*. The
stitches should be padded and
dimensional when finished, but the
ribbon should lay flat. Trim plastic
one square beyond the stitching.
Repeat for second earring.

Using plastic piece as a pattern,
cut matching felt pieces for backs.

Whipstitch edges of plastic using
one strand of 1/16-inch gold ribbon.

Thread a needle with sewing
thread. Insert needle through the
bottom point of earring from back.
Thread a large bead, then seed bead
onto the needle. Return thread
through the black bead to earring
back; secure thread on the back of
earring. Glue felt to back of earrings;
let dry. Attach earring clip backs or
posts to felt using cement.

★★★ **MUSICAL-
NOTE BUTTONS**
As shown on page 31.
MATERIALS *for four buttons*
Fabric
6x6-inch piece of 36-count white
Edinborough linen
Threads
Cotton embroidery floss in colors
listed in key
Blending filament in colors listed
in key

Supplies
Needle
Embroidery hoop
Magnifier (optional)
Basting thread
Button forms in the desired sizes

INSTRUCTIONS
Tape or zigzag edges of fabric.
Divide fabric into quarters using

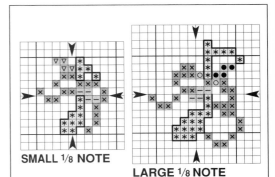

SMALL 1/8 NOTE   LARGE 1/8 NOTE

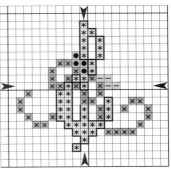

TREBLE CLEF

MUSICAL-NOTE BUTTONS

ANCHOR		DMC	
9046	⊠	321	Christmas red
228	●	700	Medium Christmas green
227	▽	701	True Christmas green
238	⊟	703	Chartreuse
	◯	001	Kreinik silver blending filament
	✶	002	Kreinik gold blending filament

BACKSTITCH
403 ╱ 310 Black –all stitches
SMALL 1/8 NOTE stitch count: 10 high x 9 wide
SMALL 1/8 NOTE finished design sizes:
36-count fabric – 1/4 x 1/4 inch
32-count fabric – 3/4 x 3/4 inch
28-count fabric – 3/8 x 3/8 inch

LARGE 1/8 NOTE stitch count: 14 high x 12 wide
LARGE 1/8 NOTE finished design sizes:
36-count fabric – 3/8 x 1/3 inch
32-count fabric – 3/8 x 3/8 inch
28-count fabric – 1/2 x 3/8 inch

TREBLE CLEF stitch count: 17 high x 17 wide
TREBLE CLEF finished design sizes:
36-count fabric – 1/2 x 1/2 inch
32-count fabric – 5/8 x 5/8 inch
28-count fabric – 3/5 x 3/5 inch

basting stitches. Find the center of
the chart and the center of one quad-
rant of the fabric; begin stitching
there. Use one ply of floss or one
strand of filament to work the cross-
stitches and backstitches over one
thread. Repeat for the other three
buttons using the remaining quad-
rants of fabric.

Press the linen on the wrong side,
using very little pressure so as not to
flatten the stitching. Center the
design over the button form; trim the
fabric ½ inch beyond the edge. Run a
gathering thread ¼ inch from the
edge. Pull the thread to smooth the
linen around the form. Assemble the
button back following the manufacturer's instructions.

★★ CELESTIAL BUTTON COVERS

*As shown on page 31, button covers are
1¼ x 1¼ inches.*

MATERIALS *for each button cover*

Fabric
3x3-inch piece of 14-count clear
perforated plastic
2x2-inch piece of dark blue felt

Threads
Kreinik midnight 060 #16 braid
Kreinik gold 002 ¹⁄₁₆-inch-wide
ribbon

Supplies
Needle; sewing thread
Seed beads in colors listed in
the key
Button cover forms (available in
the jewelry section of crafts
stores)
All-purpose cement

INSTRUCTIONS

Find center of perforated plastic
and center of desired chart; begin
stitching there. Use one strand of
braid to work the half cross-stitches.
Attach beads with needle and sewing
thread. Trim the plastic one square
beyond stitching. Cut felt back to
match button cover front. Using one
strand of gold ribbon, overcast the
edges of plastic. Glue felt to back of
stitched plastic. Attach button cover
forms to back using cement. Off-set
button cover form slightly to top of
design to prevent it from turning.

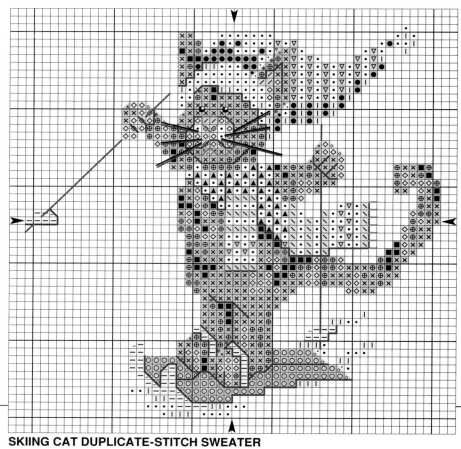

SKIING CAT DUPLICATE-STITCH SWEATER

ANCHOR		DMC	
002	⊡	000	White
110	●	208	Dark lavender
108	▽	210	Light lavender
352	■	300	Deep mahogany
289	−	307	Lemon
1047	☒	402	Pale mahogany
890	○	729	Old gold
160	‖	827	Powder blue
229	▲	910	Emerald
338	⊕	921	Copper
187	⧵	992	Aquamarine
886	◇	3047	Yellow beige
031	⧸	3708	Watermelon

BACKSTITCH

847	╱	3072	Beaver gray—whiskers, ski poles
031	╱	3708	Watermelon—nose, mouth, fringe on scarf
360	╱	3031	Mocha—all remaining stitches

STRAIGHT STITCH

403	╱	310	Black—whiskers

FRENCH KNOT

002	○	000	White—eye
403	●	310	Black—eye

Stitch count: 51 high x 52 wide
Finished design sizes:
14-count fabric – 3⅝ x 3⅝ inches
8½-count fabric – 6 x 6 inches

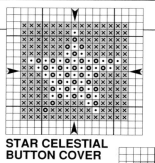

STAR CELESTIAL BUTTON COVER

MOON CELESTIAL BUTTON COVER

CELESTIAL BUTTON COVERS

CONTINENTAL STITCH

☒ 060 Kreinik midnight
medium #16 braid

BEADS

⊡ 02010 Mill Hill ice seed bead
◉ 02011 Mill Hill Victorian gold
seed bead

MOON stitch count: 15 high x 15 wide
MOON finished design size:
14-count fabric – 1 x 1 inch

STAR stitch count: 14 high x 15 wide
STAR finished design size:
14-count fabric – 1 x 1 inch

PAWS–SKIING CAT SWEATER

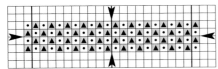

BORDER–SKIING CAT SWEATER

★ SKIING CAT DUPLICATE-STITCH SWEATER

As shown on page 32.

MATERIALS

Fabric

Purchased red cotton stockinette-stitch crew neck sweater with a gauge of 7 stitches and 10 rows = 1 inch

Floss

Cotton embroidery floss in colors listed in key on page 40

Supplies

Measuring tape

Tapestry needle

Six ⁵⁄₈-inch-wide acrylic snowflake beads

Six 2-millimeter pearls

Two ¹⁄₄-inch-diameter pom-poms

INSTRUCTIONS

Find the vertical center of the sweater front; sew a line of basting stitches from the top to the bottom. Mark a point 3 inches below the lower edge of the neck band along the basting; begin stitching center top of cat's hat there.

Use six plies of floss for all the duplicate stitches. Work the remaining stitches using three plies of floss. For the eyes, make the black French knots with three plies of floss, then white French knot with two plies of floss. Use two plies to attach the snowflake beads, placing a pearl in the center. Tack the pom-poms to the tip of the cap.

For sleeves, measure ³⁄₄ inch from the top of the ribbing, begin stitching the border motif there. Randomly stitch paw prints going up and down on one sleeve of the sweater.

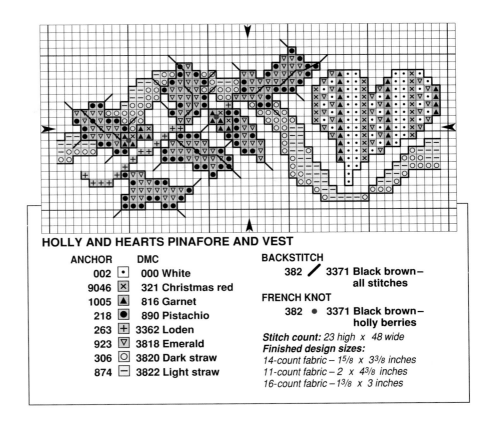

HOLLY AND HEARTS PINAFORE AND VEST

ANCHOR		DMC		BACKSTITCH
002	•	000	White	382 ╱ 3371 Black brown– all stitches
9046	✕	321	Christmas red	
1005	▲	816	Garnet	**FRENCH KNOT**
218	●	890	Pistachio	382 ● 3371 Black brown– holly berries
263	+	3362	Loden	
923	▽	3818	Emerald	*Stitch count:* 23 high x 48 wide
306	○	3820	Dark straw	*Finished design sizes:*
874	–	3822	Light straw	14-count fabric – 1⁵⁄₈ x 3³⁄₈ inches
				11-count fabric – 2 x 4³⁄₈ inches
				16-count fabric – 1³⁄₈ x 3 inches

HOLLY AND HEARTS PINAFORE AND VEST

As shown on page 33.

★★★ HOLLY AND HEARTS PINAFORE

MATERIALS

Fabrics

Purchased white pinafore

3-inch-wide piece of 14-count waste canvas same length as the hemline

Floss

Cotton embroidery floss in colors listed in key

Supplies

Needle

Basting thread

Tweezers

INSTRUCTIONS

Tape the edges of the canvas. Baste canvas around the hemline with the edge of canvas even with hem. Find the vertical center of the skirt, canvas, and center of the chart; begin stitching there. Use three plies of cotton embroidery floss for the cross-stitches and one ply of floss for the French knots and backstitches.

Remove the basting threads; trim the canvas close to the stitching. Wet the canvas slightly. Using the

tweezers, pull the canvas from under the cross-stitches.

★★ HOLLY VEST

MATERIALS

Fabrics

Purchased red vest

4x3¹⁄₂-inch piece of 14-count waste canvas

Floss

Cotton embroidery floss in colors listed in key

Supplies

Needle

Basting thread

Tweezers

INSTRUCTIONS

Tape the edges of the canvas to prevent fraying. Baste the waste canvas to the right side of vest with top of canvas 4¹⁄₂ inches from the shoulder seam, centered side to side. Use three plies of floss to work the cross-stitches; use one ply of floss for French knots and backstitches.

Remove basting threads and trim the canvas close to stitching. Wet canvas slightly. Using the tweezers, pull individual threads from under the cross-stitches.

FESTIVE HOLIDAY GREETINGS

*Y*ou know Christmas is coming when the decorations are brought out for display. This stunning treasury of designs will welcome holiday guests in style, each making a generous and thoughtful gift.

Stitch this shimmering *Noel Ribbon* with ease on 28-count harvest autumn linen. Add a pretty ribbon rose bow and tassels for an elegant finish. Complete instructions and chart are on page 49.

Designer: Barbara Sestok
Photographer: Scott Little

Santa Cardholder

What better way to display your cards than in this clever cardholder?
Fuzzy novelty thread provides additional sparkle to this
charming Santa. The design is stitched in two sections, then assembled
pillowcase-style. Instructions and charts begin on page 49.

Designer: Bette Ashley ◆ Photographer: Hopkins Associates

Noel Bell Pull

Metallic gold thread and cotton floss transform Aida banding into a quick-to-stitch holiday decoration. The design is worked in whole stitches for a last-minute gift that's perfect for everyone on your list. Instructions and chart begin on page 52.

Designer: Alice Okon
Photographer: Hopkins Associates

Peace Sampler

Echoing the sentiment of this joyous season, our miniature sampler makes an elegant gift. The 28-count black Jobelan lends a dramatic flair to the simple lines of this design. Use gold and red velvet double matting to create a rich and festive appearance. Instructions and chart are on page 53.

Designer: Ursula Michael
Photographer: Hopkins Associates

Christmas Greetings Sampler

Christmas is a holiday known and celebrated in different ways around the world. Create this joyous sampler on 28-count white linen to spread the cheer in all languages. Complete instructions and chart begin on page 54.

Designer: Linda Gordanier Jary ◆ Photographer: Scott Little

Twelve Days of Christmas Quilt and Ornaments

Adorn your wall with this heartwarming *Twelve Days of Christmas Quilt*. Each motif stitches up quickly on 14-count white Aida cloth and then is pieced together with a fun red-and-green Christmas tree fabric. Create all the motifs as ornaments to hang on your tree, around a wreath, or displayed throughout your holiday home. The complete instructions and charts are on pages 56–63.

Designer: Lorri Birmingham
Photographer: Scott Little

A PARTRIDGE IN A PEAR TREE

TWO TURTLE DOVES

THREE FRENCH HENS

FOUR CALLING BIRDS

FIVE GOLD RINGS

SIX GEESE LAYING

SEVEN SWANS SWIMMING

EIGHT MAIDS MILKING

NINE LADIES DANCING

TEN LORDS LEAPING

ELEVEN PIPERS PIPING

TWELVE DRUMMERS DRUMMING

Christmas Cheer Sampler

The traditional colors of Christmas are used to create this simple
stitchery worked on 32-count white linen. This piece is bordered with good little
boy and girl motifs, and will add seasonal charm to any home. Complete
instructions and chart are on pages 64–65.

Designer: Patricia Andrle ◆ Photographer: Scott Little

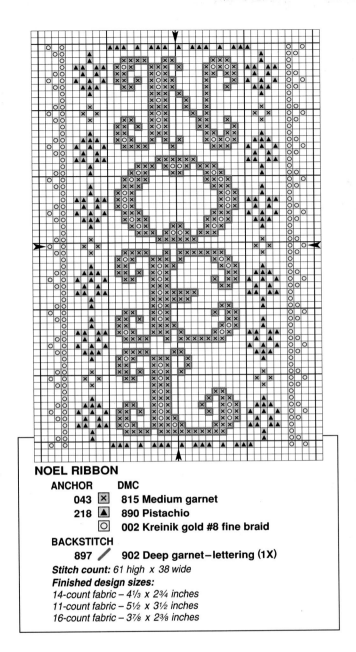

NOEL RIBBON

ANCHOR		DMC
043	☒	815 Medium garnet
218	▲	890 Pistachio
	⊙	002 Kreinik gold #8 fine braid

BACKSTITCH

897	╱	902 Deep garnet–lettering (1X)

Stitch count: 61 high x 38 wide
Finished design sizes:
14-count fabric – 4⅓ x 2¾ inches
11-count fabric – 5½ x 3½ inches
16-count fabric – 3⅞ x 2⅜ inches

★★ NOEL RIBBON

As shown on page 42, finished ribbon is 2⅞ inches wide.

MATERIALS

Fabrics

5-inch-wide piece of 28-count harvest autumn linen in desired length
2½-inch-wide piece of white lightweight fusible interfacing in desired length

Threads

Cotton embroidery floss in colors listed in key; #8 gold braid

Supplies

Needle
Embroidery hoop

INSTRUCTIONS

Tape or zigzag edges of fabric. Find vertical center of chart and vertical center of fabric. Measure 1 inch from one end of linen strip; begin stitching there. Use three plies floss or one strand braid to work cross-stitches over two threads. Stitch the pattern until the desired length is reached. Center design; trim linen to measure 3⅞ inches wide. Trim the short ends 1 inch from stitching.

Press edges under ½ inch on all sides. Center interfacing on back of stitchery with interfacing over pressed edges. Fuse following the manufacturer's instructions.

★★★ SANTA CARDHOLDER

As shown on page 43, cardholder is 28x15¾ inches.

MATERIALS

Fabrics

36x24-inch piece of 7-count cream country Aida
16x24-inch piece of 7-count cream country Aida
30x18-inch piece of fusible fleece
⅝ yard of hunter green polished cotton
⅓ yard white fusible interfacing
⅓ yard of white fabric

Threads

Cotton embroidery floss in colors listed in key on page 50
Novelty threads in colors listed in key on page 50

Supplies

Needle; embroidery hoop
2½ yards of ½-inch-diameter purchased hunter green piping
27x14½-inch piece of foam mounting board
1-inch-diameter gold star sequin
One ¼-inch-diameter red bead
Twenty ⅜-inch-diameter brass bells
1 yard of ⅛-inch-wide hunter green ribbon
1 yard of ⅛-inch-wide emerald green ribbon
Ten 10-inch pieces of ⅛-inch-diameter burgundy satin ribbon
15-inch-long wood decorator dowel
27-inch-long burgundy tasseled drapery cord
27-inch-long hunter green tasseled drapery cord

INSTRUCTIONS

Tape or zigzag the edges of the 36x24-inch piece of Aida cloth to prevent it from fraying. Find the vertical center of the cardholder chart and the vertical center of the fabric. Measure 4 inches from the top of the Aida cloth; begin stitching top border there. Use six plies of floss to work all the cross-stitches. Work backstitches using two plies of floss or one strand of novelty thread unless otherwise specified in the key on page 50.

For pocket, find the vertical center of the pocket chart and the vertical center of the remaining Aida fabric. Measure 3 inches from the top of fabric; begin stitching the top border there. Work all the stitches as for cardholder. Attach the sequin and bead using two plies of matching floss. Trim cardholder to 28½x16 inches and pocket to 11x16 inches. Set aside.

From hunter green fabric, cut an 18x30-inch back and a 2½x16½-inch hanging strip. All the measurements include a ½-inch seam allowance. All seams are sewn together with the right sides facing unless it is otherwise specified.

Fuse the interfacing to the back of the pocket following manufacturer's instructions. Trim the pocket ⅝ inch from stitching on all four sides. Use the pocket as a pattern to cut a lining piece from the white fabric. Sew the pocket and lining together

½ inch from top edge. Press lining to back of pocket.

Center the fusible fleece on the back of the Santa design. Fuse following the manufacturer's instructions. Position the top edge of the pocket 1 inch below the bottom row of the Santa motif, raw edges even, and aligning the side border of the cardholder with the side border of the pocket; baste.

Trim the top and the sides of the cardholder ⅝ inch from the border stitching. Pin the piping around the perimeter of the cardholder with the right sides together and raw edges even. Sew close to cording, using a zipper foot.

For dowel hanging strip, fold both short ends of the strip under 1 inch; press. Fold strip in half lengthwise with wrong sides together. Center strip along top edge of the cardholder, raw edges even. Use zipper foot to sew close to cord.

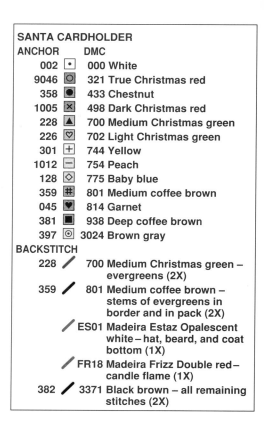

SANTA CARDHOLDER

ANCHOR		DMC	
002	·	000	White
9046	O	321	True Christmas red
358	●	433	Chestnut
1005	✕	498	Dark Christmas red
228	▲	700	Medium Christmas green
226	♡	702	Light Christmas green
301	+	744	Yellow
1012	−	754	Peach
128	◇	775	Baby blue
359	#	801	Medium coffee brown
045	♥	814	Garnet
381	■	938	Deep coffee brown
397	⊙	3024	Brown gray

BACKSTITCH

228	/	700	Medium Christmas green – evergreens (2X)
359	/	801	Medium coffee brown – stems of evergreens in border and in pack (2X)
	/	ES01	Madeira Estaz Opalescent white – hat, beard, and coat bottom (1X)
	/	FR18	Madeira Frizz Double red – candle flame (1X)
382	/	3371	Black brown – all remaining stitches (2X)

SANTA CARDHOLDER POCKET

Pocket stitch count: 69 high x 102 wide
Finished design sizes:
7-count fabric – 9⅞ x 14⅝ inches
11-count fabric – 6⅓ x 9⅓ inches
14-count fabric – 5 x 7⅓ inches

SANTA CARDHOLDER

Santa stitch count: 134 high x 102 wide
Finished design sizes:
7-count fabric – 19⅛ x 14⅝ inches
11-count fabric – 12¼ x 9⅓ inches
14-count fabric – 9⅔ x 7⅓ inches

51

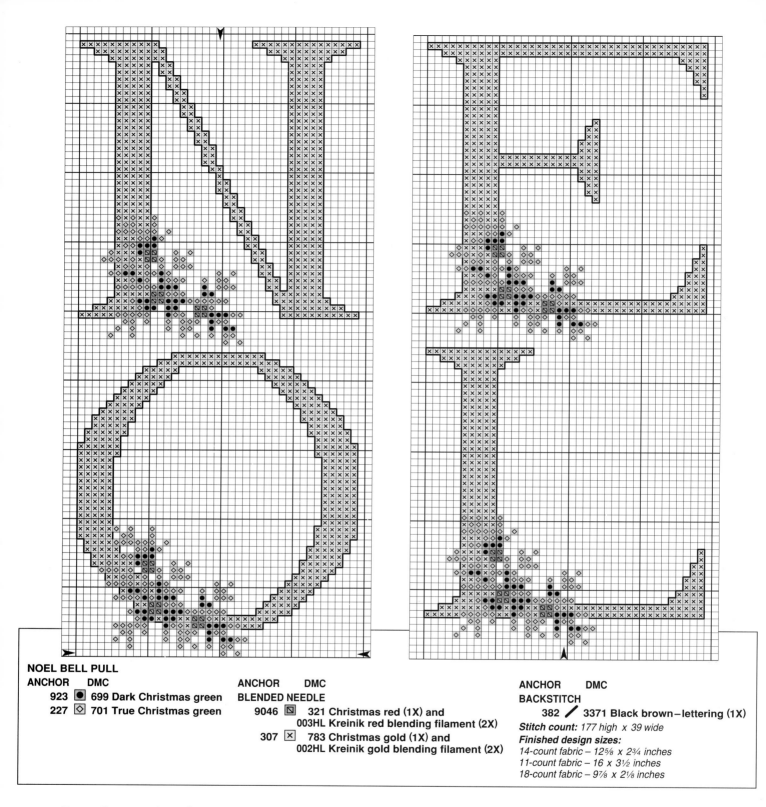

NOEL BELL PULL

ANCHOR	DMC		ANCHOR	DMC		ANCHOR	DMC
923 ●	699 Dark Christmas green			BLENDED NEEDLE			BACKSTITCH
227 ◇	701 True Christmas green		9046 ☒	321 Christmas red (1X) and 003HL Kreinik red blending filament (2X)		382 ╱	3371 Black brown – lettering (1X)
			307 ☒	783 Christmas gold (1X) and 002HL Kreinik gold blending filament (2X)			

Stitch count: 177 high x 39 wide
Finished design sizes:
14-count fabric – 12⅝ x 2¾ inches
11-count fabric – 16 x 3½ inches
18-count fabric – 9⅞ x 2⅛ inches

Press the top edge of the back piece under ½ inch. Sew the cardholder front to back with the right sides together and the raw edges even along the sides and the bottom, leaving top open. Turn right side out and press. Insert the foam board into the opening at the top of the cardholder. Whipstitch back to the stitching line of the hanging strip to close. Insert dowel through hanger strip. Join the ends of burgundy and green drapery cords. Tie ends of cords around each end of dowel rod.

Join the ends of the green ribbons and tie into a bow. Tack the bow to the bottom of the lantern. Tie jingle bells onto the ends of the burgundy ribbon pieces. Join two ribbons together and tie a bow. Repeat to make four more bows. Tack the bows to the cardholder, referring to the photograph on page 43 for placement.

★★ NOEL BELL PULL

As shown on page 44, bell pull is 16 inches long.

MATERIALS

Fabrics

17-inch piece of 14-count white
   4⅝-inch-wide Aida banding
   with gold star edge
4⅜×15½-inch piece of
   lightweight fusible interfacing

Threads

Cotton embroidery floss and
   filament listed in key, *opposite*

Supplies

Needle
Embroidery hoop
5-inch-wide brass bell pull
   hardware
1 yard of 1½-inch-wide white
   print wire-edged ribbon

INSTRUCTIONS

Topstitch ¾ inch from cut edge
on both ends of the banding. Find
the vertical center of chart. Measure
2¾ inches from one end of the
banding. Begin stitching top row of
"N" there. Use three plies of floss to
work all cross-stitches. Work the
blended needle as specified in the
key. Work all the backstitches using
one ply of floss.

Fuse the interfacing to the back
of the banding following the manufacturer's instructions with the
bottom edge of the interfacing even
with the topstitching at the bottom
of the band. Fold the top edge of
banding ¼-inch toward the back;
stitch.

Place the bell-pull holder inside
the fold and hand stitch the
folded edge to the back of the
design fabric.

To fringe, remove the threads
between the bottom cut edge and
the topstitching. Tie the ribbon bow
at the top of hardware.

★ PEACE SAMPLER

As shown on page 44.

MATERIALS

Fabric

11×9-inch piece of 28-count
   black Jobelan fabric

Floss

Cotton embroidery floss in colors
   listed in key

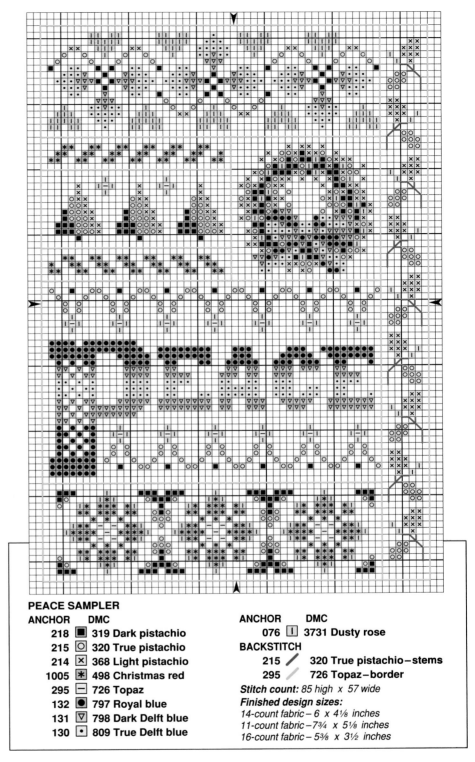

PEACE SAMPLER

ANCHOR		DMC	
218	■	319	Dark pistachio
215	◎	320	True pistachio
214	✕	368	Light pistachio
1005	✳	498	Christmas red
295	−	726	Topaz
132	●	797	Royal blue
131	▽	798	Dark Delft blue
130	·	809	True Delft blue

ANCHOR		DMC	
076	Ι	3731	Dusty rose

BACKSTITCH

215	╱	320 True pistachio–stems
295	╱	726 Topaz–border

Stitch count: 85 high x 57 wide
Finished design sizes:
14-count fabric – 6 x 4⅛ inches
11-count fabric – 7¾ x 5⅛ inches
16-count fabric – 5⅜ x 3½ inches

Supplies

Needle
Embroidery hoop
Desired frame and mat

INSTRUCTIONS

Tape or zigzag the edges of the
28-count black Jobelan fabric to
prevent it from fraying. Find the
center of the chart and the center of
the fabric; begin stitching there. Use
three plies of cotton embroidery floss
to work all the cross-stitches over
two threads of fabric. Work the backstitches using two plies of embroidery floss. Press the finished stitchery from the back. Mat and frame the
piece as desired.

54

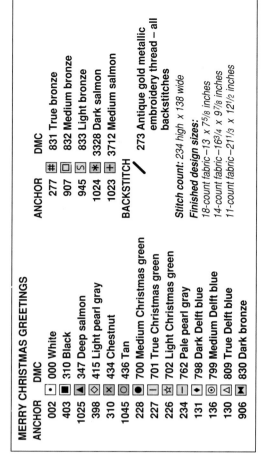

MERRY CHRISTMAS GREETINGS

ANCHOR		DMC	
002	•	000	White
403	■	310	Black
1025	◄	347	Deep salmon
398	◇	415	Light pearl gray
310	✕	434	Chestnut
1045	○	436	Tan
228	●	700	Medium Christmas green
227	—	701	True Christmas green
226	☆	702	Light Christmas green
234	❘	762	Pale pearl gray
131	◆	798	Dark Delft blue
136	◉	799	Medium Delft blue
130	△	809	True Delft blue
906	✕	830	Dark bronze

ANCHOR		DMC	
277	#	831	True bronze
907	□	832	Medium bronze
945	◩	833	Light bronze
1024	✳	3328	Dark salmon
1023	+	3712	Medium salmon
BACKSTITCH			
273	⁄		Antique gold metallic embroidery thread – all backstitches

Stitch count: 234 high x 138 wide
Finished design sizes:
18-count fabric–13 x 7⅝ inches
14-count fabric–16¾ x 9⅞ inches
11-count fabric–21⅓ x 12½ inches

★★ MERRY CHRISTMAS GREETINGS

As shown on page 45.

MATERIALS
Fabric
13x20-inch piece of 28-count white linen

Threads
Cotton embroidery floss in colors listed in key
Metallic embroidery thread in color listed in key

Supplies
Needle
Embroidery hoop
Desired frame and mat

INSTRUCTIONS
Tape or zigzag edges of fabric to prevent fraying. Find the center of the chart and the center of the fabric; begin stitching there. Use three plies of floss to work cross-stitches over two threads of fabric. Work backstitches using one strand of metallic thread. Press from the back. Mat and frame as desired.

★★★★ TWELVE DAYS OF CHRISTMAS QUILT

As shown on page 47, the quilt is 38¾x30¼ inches.

MATERIALS
Fabrics
Twelve 9x9-inch pieces of 14-count white Aida cloth
¼ yard of 45-inch-wide red Christmas tree print fabric
½ yard of 45-inch-wide green Christmas tree print fabric
⅔ yard of 45-inch-wide solid green fabric
1⅛ yard of polyester quilt batting

Threads
Cotton embroidery floss in colors listed in key on pages 62–63
Blending filament in color listed in key on pages 62–63

Supplies
Needle; embroidery hoop
Matching sewing thread

INSTRUCTIONS
Tape or zigzag edges of fabric to prevent fraying. Find center of desired chart and center of one Aida square; begin stitching there. Use three plies of floss to work cross-stitches. Work the French knots using two plies unless otherwise specified. Work half cross-stitches using two plies and blended needles as specified in the key. Work all of the backstitches using one ply of floss. Work each of the charts. Trim Aida cloth squares to measure 6½x6½-inches and set aside.

From green tree-print fabric, cut twenty-four 1⅜x6½-inch vertical sashing strips, and twenty-four 1⅜x8¼-inch horizontal sashing strips. From the solid green fabric, cut eight 1⅝x8¼-inch vertical sashing strips, five 1⅝x26-inch joining strips, and two 1⅝x37½-inch side borders. From red tree-print fabric, cut one 35½x43½-inch quilt back. All measurements include ¼-inch seam allowances. All seams are sewn with the right sides together unless it is otherwise specified.

Sew a green tree vertical sashing strip to each side of each Aida square. Sew a green tree horizontal sashing strip to top and bottom of each square to complete each block.

Sew a solid green vertical sashing strip to the right edge of the partridge block. Sew the opposite edge of the sashing strip to the left edge of the turtle dove block. Sew a second vertical sashing strip to the right edge of the turtle dove block. Sew the opposite edge of the second sashing strip to the left edge of the French hens block to complete the first row of quilt blocks. Set aside.

Continue to join the squares and sashing in this manner to make four rows, positioning the blocks in numerical order.

Sew one long edge of the green joining strip to the bottom edge of the first row of blocks. Sew the remaining long edge of the strip to the top edge of the second row. Continue to join rows in this manner. Sew the remaining joining strips to the top and the bottom edges of the quilt. Sew a side border strip to each side of the quilt.

Layer the red tree quilt back, the batting, and the quilt top. Baste the layers together close to the seam lines. With the red thread in the bobbin and the white thread in the needle, stitch in the ditch around each of the Aida cloth squares. With the red thread in the bobbin and the green thread in the needle, machine-quilt in each of the seam lines of the quilt top.

Press the raw edges of the quilt back under ¼-inch. Fold the edges of the quilt back to the front of the quilt; miter the corners. With the red thread in both the bobbin and the needle, sew in place close to the folded edges.

★★★★ TWELVE DAYS OF CHRISTMAS ORNAMENTS

As shown on page 46, ornaments are 6¾x6¾ inches.

MATERIALS *for each ornament*
Fabrics
8x8-inch piece of 18-count white Aida cloth
Two 2½x5-inch pieces of red or green Christmas print fabric
Two 2½x8½-inch pieces of red or green Christmas print fabric
6⅜x6⅜-inch piece of red felt

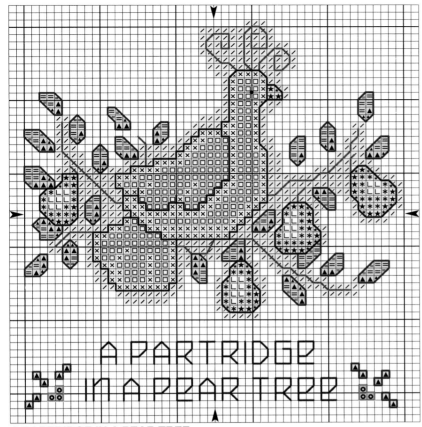

A PARTRIDGE IN A PEAR TREE

Partridge in a pear tree stitch count: 53 high x 50 wide
Partridge in a pear tree finished design sizes:
14-count fabric – 3⅞ x 3⅝ inches
11-count fabric – 4⅞ x 4⅝ inches
18-count fabric – 3 x 2⅞ inches

TWO TURTLE DOVES

Two turtle doves stitch count: 42 high x 54 wide
Two turtle doves finished design sizes:
14-count fabric – 3 x 3⅞ inches
11-count fabric – 3⅞ x 5 inches
18-count fabric – 2⅓ x 3 inches

Floss

Cotton embroidery floss in colors listed in key on pages 62–63
Blending filament in colors listed in key on pages 62–63

Supplies

Needle; embroidery hoop
6½ x 6½-inch piece of self-stick mounting board with foam
27-inch piece of ¼-inch-diameter red or green cord
10-inch piece of ¼-inch-diameter red or green cord
10-inch piece of 2⅞-inch-wide red-and-green wire-edged ribbon
2½-inch piece of ¼-inch-wide metallic gold ribbon
Crafts glue

INSTRUCTIONS

Tape or zigzag edges of fabric to prevent fraying. Find center of desired chart and center of one piece of Aida; begin stitching there. Use two plies of floss to work cross-stitches, half cross-stitches, and French knots. Work blended needle as specified in key. Work backstitches using one ply of floss. Trim Aida squares to 5x5 inches; set aside.

Cut two 2½ x 5-inch vertical side sashing strips and two 2½ x 8½-inch horizontal top and bottom sashing strips from red or green Christmas print fabric.

Sew a vertical sashing strip to each side of the Aida square. Sew a horizontal sashing strip to the top and bottom edge of each square to complete the block.

Peel the protective paper from mounting board. Center the foam mounting board on the back of the stitchery and press to stick. Trim the fabric ½ inch beyond mounting board. Fold the excess fabric to the back, mitering corners, and glue.

Position and glue the cord around front edges of ornament, overlapping ends at bottom, and glue edges to back. Glue ends of the 10 inch cord to top corners of ornament. Join the ends of the red-and-green ribbon to make a continuous circle. With the joined ends at the center, gather center of ribbon through both layers. Wrap the gold ribbon over gathered center and secure.

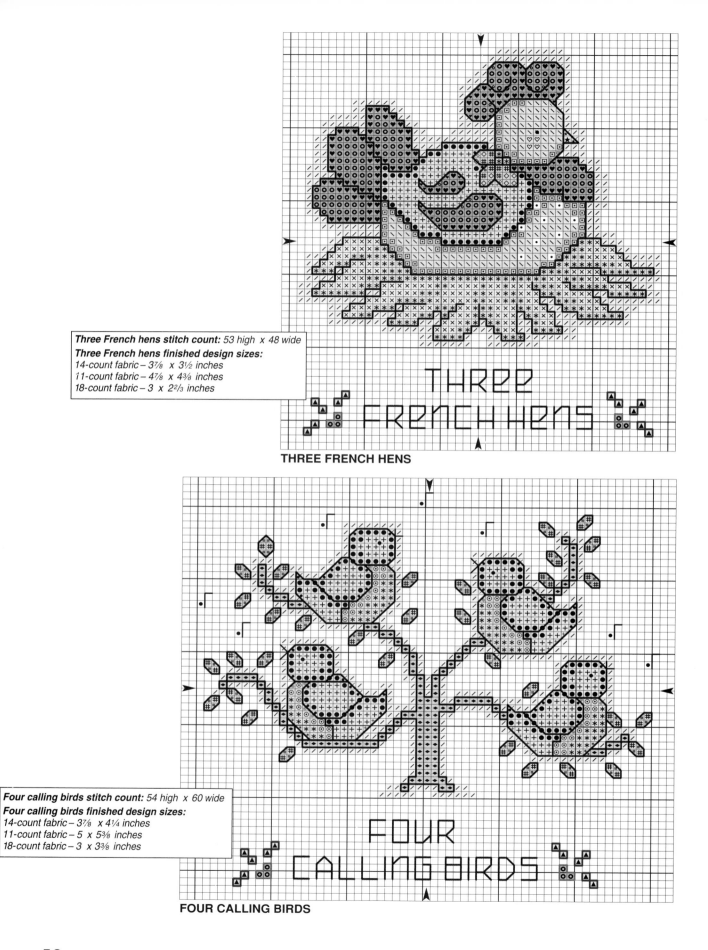

Three French hens stitch count: 53 high x 48 wide
Three French hens finished design sizes:
14-count fabric – 3⅞ x 3½ inches
11-count fabric – 4⅞ x 4⅜ inches
18-count fabric – 3 x 2⅔ inches

THREE FRENCH HENS

Four calling birds stitch count: 54 high x 60 wide
Four calling birds finished design sizes:
14-count fabric – 3⅞ x 4¼ inches
11-count fabric – 5 x 5⅜ inches
18-count fabric – 3 x 3⅜ inches

FOUR CALLING BIRDS

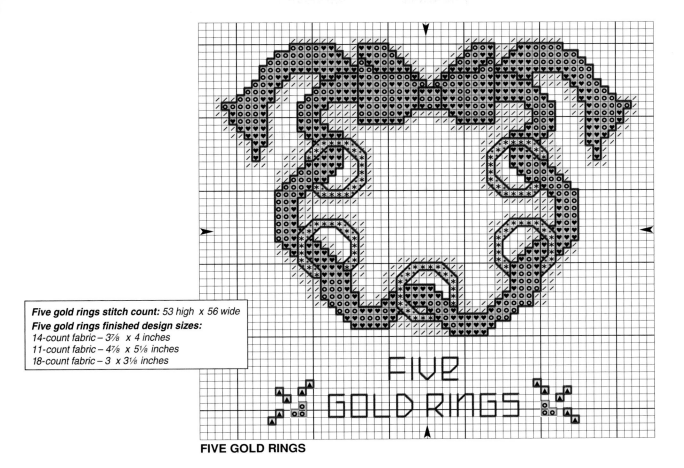

Five gold rings stitch count: *53 high x 56 wide*
Five gold rings finished design sizes:
14-count fabric – 3⅞ x 4 inches
11-count fabric – 4⅞ x 5⅛ inches
18-count fabric – 3 x 3⅛ inches

FIVE GOLD RINGS

Six geese laying stitch count: *61 high x 45 wide*
Six geese laying finished design sizes:
14-count fabric – 4⅜ x 3¼ inches
11-count fabric – 5⅝ x 4⅛ inches
18-count fabric – 3½ x 2½ inches

SIX GEESE LAYING

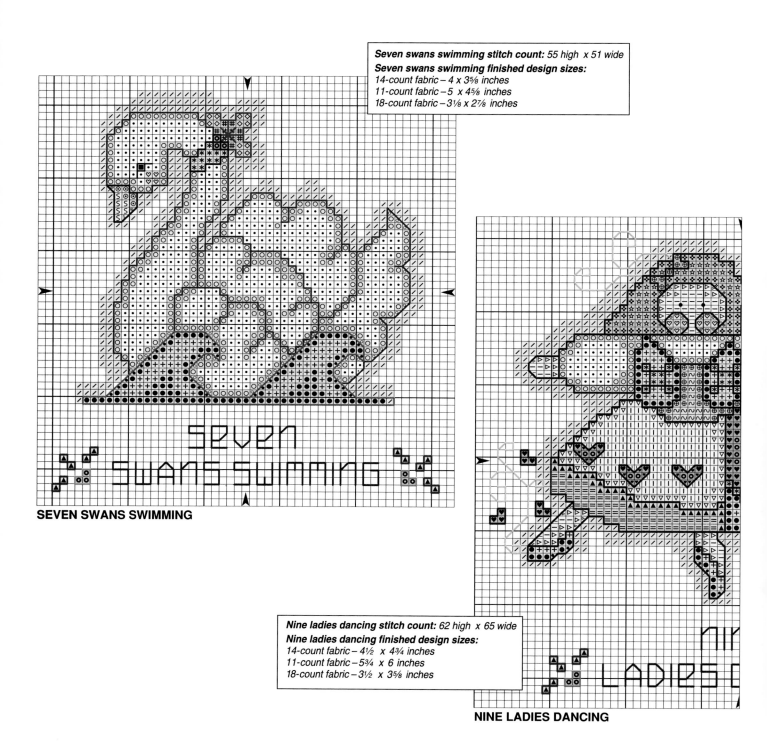

Seven swans swimming stitch count: *55 high x 51 wide*
Seven swans swimming finished design sizes:
14-count fabric – 4 x 3⅝ inches
11-count fabric – 5 x 4⅝ inches
18-count fabric – 3⅛ x 2⅞ inches

SEVEN SWANS SWIMMING

Nine ladies dancing stitch count: *62 high x 65 wide*
Nine ladies dancing finished design sizes:
14-count fabric – 4½ x 4¾ inches
11-count fabric – 5¾ x 6 inches
18-count fabric – 3½ x 3⅝ inches

NINE LADIES DANCING

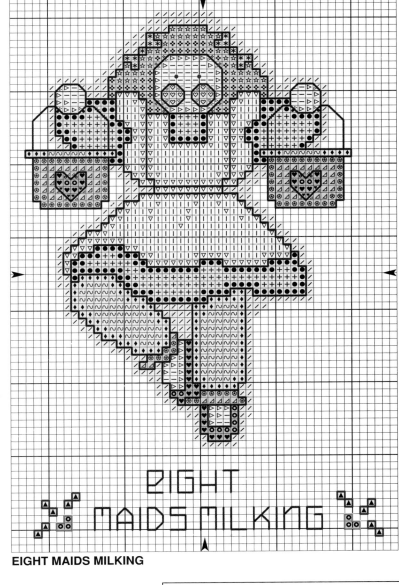

EIGHT MAIDS MILKING

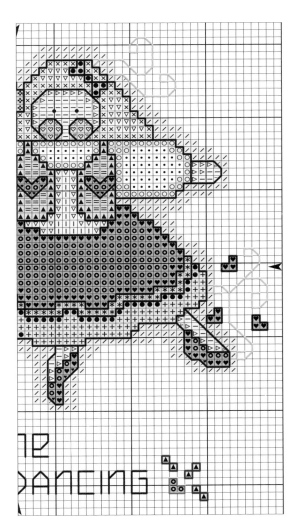

Eight maids milking stitch count: 72 high x 47 wide
Eight maids milking finished design sizes:
14-count fabric – 5¼ x 3⅜ inches
11-count fabric – 6⅝ x 4¼ inches
18-count fabric – 4 x 2⅝ inches

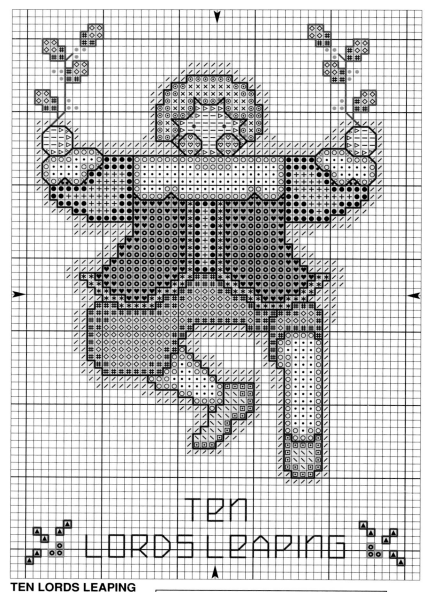

TEN LORDS LEAPING

Ten lords leaping stitch count: 74 high x 50 wide
Ten lords leaping finished design sizes:
14-count fabric – 5⅜ x 3⅝ inches
11-count fabric – 6¾ x 4⅝ inches
18-count fabric – 4⅛ x 2⅞ inches

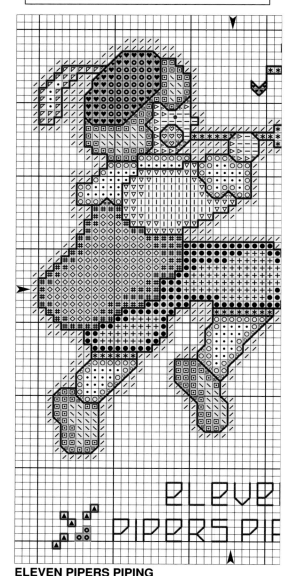

Eleven pipers piping stitch count: 71 high x 53 wide
Eleven pipers piping finished design sizes:
14-count fabric – 5⅛ x 3⅞ inches
11-count fabric – 6½ x 4⅞ inches
18-count fabric – 4 x 3 inches

ELEVEN PIPERS PIPING

TWELVE DAYS OF CHRISTMAS

ANCHOR	DMC		ANCHOR	DMC		ANCHOR	DMC	
002	000	White	877	502	Medium blue green	160	827	Light powder blue
110	208	Dark lavender	875	503	True blue green	052	899	Light rose
109	209	Medium lavender	891	676	Light old gold	274	928	Pale gray blue
108	210	Light lavender	886	677	Pale old gold	886	3047	Light yellow beige
1006	304	Medium Christmas red	324	721	Medium bittersweet	292	3078	Pale lemon
403	310	Black	323	722	Light bittersweet	144	3325	True baby blue
400	317	True pewter	305	725	True topaz	036	3326	Pale rose
399	318	Light steel	295	726	Light topaz	267	3346	Light hunter green
977	334	Dark baby blue	890	729	Medium old gold	266	3347	Medium yellow green
401	413	Dark pewter	361	738	Light tan	1028	3685	Deep mauve
398	415	Light pearl gray	885	739	Pale tan	068	3687	True mauve
310	434	Medium chestnut	300	745	Light yellow			
1046	435	Dark chestnut	307	783	True Christmas gold		**HALF CROSS-STITCH**	
1045	436	Dark tan	144	800	Pale Delft blue		(stitch in direction of symbol)	
362	437	Medium tan	1005	816	Light garnet	848	927	Light gray blue

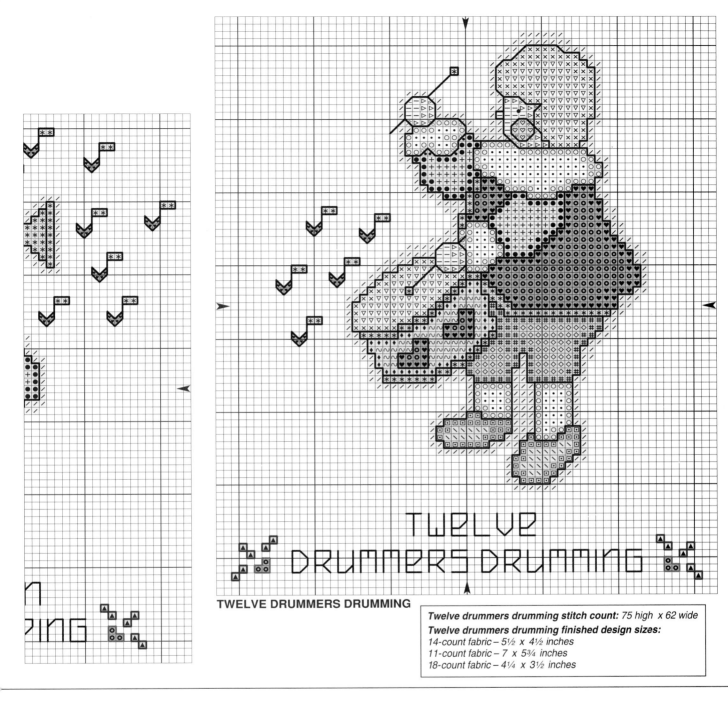

TWELVE DRUMMERS DRUMMING

Twelve drummers drumming stitch count: 75 high x 62 wide
Twelve drummers drumming finished design sizes:
14-count fabric – 5½ x 4½ inches
11-count fabric – 7 x 5¾ inches
18-count fabric – 4¼ x 3½ inches

ANCHOR	DMC	
BLENDED NEEDLE		
235	414	Dark steel (2X) and 001 Kreinik silver blending filament (1X)
305	725	True topaz (2X) and 002 Kreinik gold blending filament (1X)
BACKSTITCH		
110	208	Dark lavender – hearts (doves)
1006	304	Medium Christmas red – holly berries
403	310	Black – swan eye, bird's notes and beak
979	312	Light navy – swan wave
977	334	Dark baby blue – doves

ANCHOR	DMC	
BACKSTITCH		
235	414	Dark steel – swan
310	434	Medium chestnut – partridge curls and tree
878	501	Dark blue green – doves' holly and vine
359	801	Medium coffee brown – swan beak and ribbon, maids, calling birds, rings, partridge, dancing ladies, hens, geese, lords, pipers, drummers
360	898	Dark coffee brown – doves' beak and heart
052	899	Light rose – doves' cheeks
268	3345	Medium hunter green – leaves, partridge

ANCHOR	DMC	
BACKSTITCH		
1028	3685	Deep mauve – doves' hearts
BLENDED BACKSTITCH		
305	725	True topaz (1X) and 002 Kreinik gold blending filament (1X) – ladies
FRENCH KNOT		
1006	304	Medium Christmas red – berries
403	310	Black – partridge, chicken (2X); eyes (1X)
359	801	Medium coffee brown – maid eyes (2X)
360	898	Dark coffee brown – doves' eyes (1X)
1028	3685	Deep mauve – holly (3X)

★★CHRISTMAS CHEER SAMPLER

As shown on page 48.

MATERIALS

Fabric

12 x16-inch piece of 32-count white linen

Floss

Cotton embroidery floss in colors listed in key

Supplies

Needle

Embroidery hoop

Desired frame and mat

INSTRUCTIONS

Tape or zigzag the edges of the fabric to prevent fraying. Find the center of the chart and the center of the fabric; begin stitching there. Use three plies of floss to work all the cross-stitches over two threads of fabric. Press the finished stitchery from the back. Mat and frame the piece as desired.

CHRISTMAS CHEER		
ANCHOR	**DMC**	
215	☒	320 True pistachio
1025	✳	347 Salmon
217	⊙	367 Medium pistachio
214	▽	368 Light pistachio
358	■	433 Chestnut
907	⊞	832 Bronze
1010	·	951 Ivory

Stitch count: 103 high x 151 wide

Finished design sizes:

16-count fabric – 6¼ x 9¼ inches

14-count fabric – 7⅜ x 10¾ inches

11-count fabric – 9⅜ x 13¾ inches

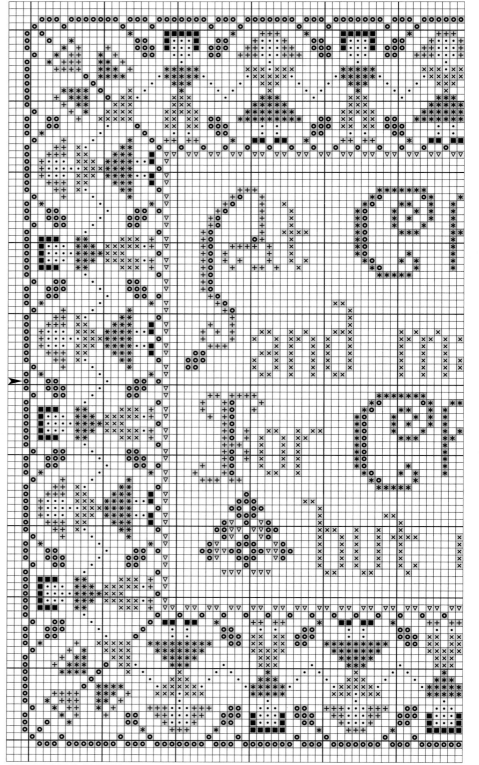

CHRISTMAS CHEER

TOKENS OF FRIENDSHIP

Stitching gifts for family and friends is a joy we all share at Christmastime. Whether big or small, each special gift means more when it is made by hand.

Embellish those personal gifts with a cross-stitched ribbon featuring a package motif. After the package is opened, the ribbon can drape through the Christmas tree as a clever garland. Instructions and chart for the *Gift-Giving Ribbon* are on page 71.

Designer: Barbara Sestok
Photographer: Scott Little

Beaded Bag and Belt Buckle

Elegance abounds this time of year, and these striking fashion accessories are no exception. The metallic stitches on this dazzling after-five bag and belt buckle glisten with shimmering beads for holiday glamour that carries over into the new year. Complete instructions and charts begin on page 71.

Designer: Alice Okon ◆ Photographer: Hopkins Associates

Holly Towel and Napkin

Use green and red embroidery floss to create this seasonal towel and napkin set that will make your holiday table more inviting. The holly leaf and berries are stitched on a 14-count ivory napkin and then repeated to make a clever border on the hand towel. The complete instructions and charts begin on page 73.

Designer: Barbara Sestok
Photographer: Scott Little

Christmas Jar Toppers

Add a tasteful touch to jars of goodies with these cheerful Christmas jar toppers. Stitch each topper on 14-count white Aida cloth, attach a colorful ruffle, and fill jars with peppermints and sugar plums for a delightful hostess gift. Complete instructions and charts begin on page 74.

Designer: Barbara Sestok
Photographer: Scott Little

Holiday Table Accessories

You can almost hear sleigh bells jingle with our place mat and napkin set stitched on 28-count red Jubilee fabric. Add smiling *Snowman Place Cards* and nut-and-candy-filled *Sleigh Party Favors* to your holiday table for the arrival of friends. Instructions and charts begin on page 75.

Designers: Jingle Bell Place Mat and Napkin, Ursula Michael; Sleigh Party Favor, Lois Winston
Photographer: Scott Little

Night Before Christmas Frame

Show off your heavenly little angel with this whimsical holiday mouse frame. The piece, stitched on 14-count white Aida cloth, uses bright colors and will be a welcoming gift for any new parent or grandparent. Complete instructions and chart begin on page 78.

Designer: Ursula Michael
Photographer: Hopkins Associates

Tree and Santa Ornaments

Stitch these three-dimensional Christmas tree ornaments using 11-count Victorian red or green Aida cloth. The use of metallic threads, seed beads, and sequins creates an extra sparkle for each ornament. The complete instructions and charts begin on page 79.

Designer: Helen Nicholson
Photographer: Hopkins Associates

★★ GIFT-GIVING RIBBON

As shown on page 66, finished ribbon is 2 inches wide.

MATERIALS

Fabrics

5-inch-wide piece of 28-count delicate pink Jobelan fabric in desired length

1¾-inch-wide piece of white lightweight fusible interfacing in desired length

Threads

Cotton embroidery floss in colors listed in key

Silver metallic embroidery thread

Supplies

Needle

Embroidery hoop

INSTRUCTIONS

Tape or zigzag edges of fabric to prevent fraying. Find the vertical center of the chart and the vertical center of the fabric. Measure 1 inch from one end of the strip; begin stitching there. Use three plies of floss to work cross-stitches over two threads of fabric. Work the French knots, straight stitches, and lazy daisy stitches as specified in the key. Work the backstitches using one ply unless otherwise specified in key. Continue stitching pattern until desired length is reached. Centering design, trim the Jobelan strip to measure 3 inches wide. Trim short ends 1 inch from the stitching.

Press edges under ½ inch on all sides of Jobelan strip. Center the interfacing on the back of stitchery with interfacing over the pressed edges of strip. Fuse following the manufacturer's instructions.

BEADED BAG AND BELT BUCKLE

As shown on page 67, bag is 5¼ x 7 inches.

★★ ELEGANT BEADED BAG

MATERIALS

Fabrics

Two 9 x 10-inch pieces of 28-count black Jobelan fabric

Two 8 x 9-inch pieces each of black cotton fabric and black fusible interfacing

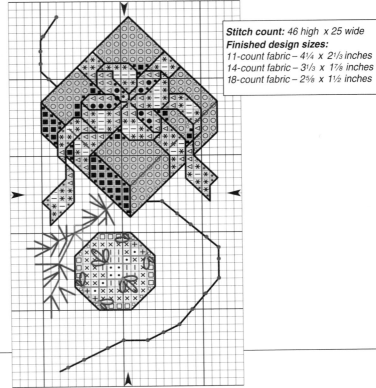

GIFT-GIVING RIBBON

ANCHOR		DMC	
002	·	000	White
9046	◁	321	True Christmas red
1005	●	498	Dark Christmas red
923	■	699	Christmas green
301	I	744	Yellow
307	□	783	Christmas gold
209	◎	912	Emerald
298	✕	972	Canary
035	✳	3705	Dark watermelon
033	−	3706	Medium watermelon
1032	✚	3752	Antique blue

BACKSTITCH

002	╱	000	White – box highlights (2X)
906	╱	829	Bronze – stem (3X)
382	╱	3371	Black brown – box, ribbon, ornament (1X); bead string (2X)

BACKSTITCH

	285	Silver metallic embroidery thread – ornament (1X)

BLENDED STRAIGHT STITCH

256	╱	906	Parrot green (1X) and
246		986	Forest green (1X) – needles

FRENCH KNOT

9046	●	321	True Christmas red – ornament (2X)
1005	●	498	Dark Christmas red – bead string (3X)

BLENDED FRENCH KNOT

9046	●	321	True Christmas red (1X) and
035		3705	Dark watermelon (1X) – bow center

LAZY DAISY

209	⬭	912	Emerald – ornament (1X)

Stitch count: 46 high x 25 wide
Finished design sizes:
11-count fabric – 4¼ x 2⅓ inches
14-count fabric – 3⅓ x 1⅞ inches
18-count fabric – 2⅝ x 1½ inches

Threads

Cotton embroidery floss in colors listed in key on page 72

#8 braid in color listed in key on page 72

Supplies

Needle

Embroidery hoop

Beading needle

Seed beads in colors listed in key on page 72

1⅝ yards of ⅛-inch-diameter black-and-gold cord

⅝ yard of ⅜-inch-wide black-and-gold sew-in piping

7-inch-long black zipper

Black sewing thread

INSTRUCTIONS

Tape or zigzag edges of one piece of Jobelan fabric to prevent fraying. Find vertical center of chart and of fabric. Measure 3¼ inches from top of fabric, begin stitching top row of center circle there. Use one strand of braid to work cross-stitches over two

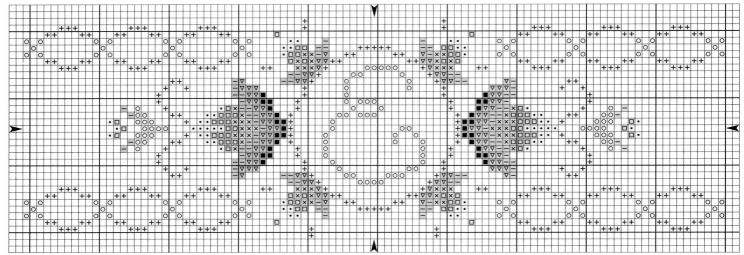

BEADED BAG AND BELT BUCKLE

threads of fabric. Use two plies of floss and half cross-stitches to attach the beads in complete rows, making the necessary color changes as they occur in rows.

Trim fabric 1¹⁄₂ inch beyond top stitching, 2¹⁄₂ inches beyond bottom stitching, and ¹⁄₂ inch beyond both sides. Use stitched piece as pattern to cut two lining pieces from black cotton and a back from remaining Jobelan fabric.

Sew piping to top straight edges of front and back bag pieces, with raw edges even and right sides together. Sew piping to bottom straight edge of bag front. Sew zipper to top edges of bag front and back. Sew the bag side seams.

Sew lining side seams. Sew lining to bag with right sides together and raw edges even. Turn lining to inside and press. Sew bag bottom and lining together along bottom piping line with wrong sides together and raw edges even. Make two 2¹⁄₂-inch loops on each end of cord; stitch to secure. Sew looped cord ends at each side of bag.

★★ **ELEGANT BEADED
BELT BUCKLE**
MATERIALS
Fabrics
6x7-inch piece of 28-count black
 Jobelan fabric
5x5-inch piece of black fusible
 interfacing
5x5-inch piece of fusible fleece
5x5-inch piece of black felt

Threads
Cotton embroidery floss as listed in
 key; #8 gold braid
Supplies
Needle; embroidery hoop
Seed beads in colors listed in key
Erasable marker; tracing paper
8x5-inch piece of perforated plastic
10¹⁄₂-inch piece of ¹⁄₈-inch-diameter
 black-and-gold cord
Purchased black belt
Crafts glue; black sewing thread

INSTRUCTIONS
Tape or zigzag the edges of the fabric to prevent fraying. Find the center of chart and the center of fabric; begin stitching there. Stitch only the center motif referring to photograph on page 67. Use one strand of braid to work all the cross-stitches over two threads of fabric. Use two plies of matching floss and half cross-stitches to attach beads in complete rows, making color changes as they occur in rows.

Use erasable marker to draw an outline ³⁄₄ inch beyond the stitching;

do not cut out. Place the tracing paper over the fabric and trace the oval outline; cut out. Use the tracing paper to cut two shapes from the perforated plastic and one shape from the felt. Fuse the interfacing to the back of the black Jobelan fabric following manufacturer's instructions.

Cut out the Jobelan oval ¹⁄₂ inch beyond the marker line. Use the stitched piece as a pattern to cut one from fleece. If necessary, remove the marker line.

Baste the plastic ovals together. Glue the fleece to the plastic, fold the excess to the back and glue. Center the stitchery over the fleece-covered shape. Run a gathering thread ¹⁄₄ inch from the cut edge; pull the gathers to smooth. Glue the edges to the back. Hand sew the black-and-gold cord around the finished oval. Overlap the ends and bring them to the back and glue. Glue the felt to the back. Whipstitch the finished oval to the purchased belt buckle. Assemble belt following the manufacturer's instructions.

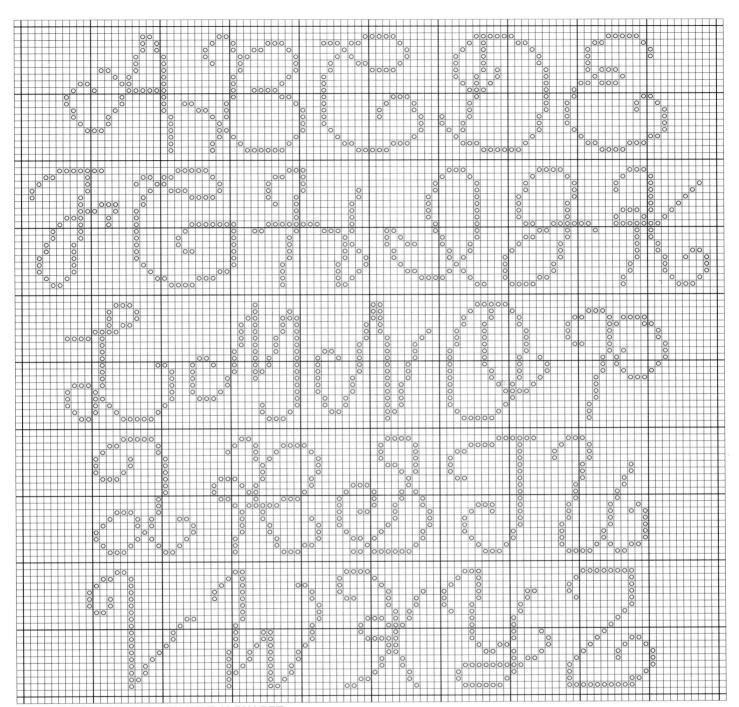

BEADED BAG AND BELT BUCKLE ALPHABET

HOLLY TOWEL AND NAPKIN

As shown on page 68.

★★★ HOLLY TOWEL

MATERIALS *for each towel*

Fabric

24½ x 14¼-inch ivory towel with a 14¼ x 3-inch-wide 14-count Aida cloth insert

Floss

Cotton embroidery floss in colors listed in key on page 74

Supplies

Needle

INSTRUCTIONS

Find the center of the chart and the center of the Aida cloth insert; begin stitching design there. Use three plies of floss to work all the cross-stitches. Work the French knots and backstitches using one ply of floss. Press the finished stitchery from the back.

★★ HOLLY NAPKIN

MATERIALS

For each napkin

Fabric

15 x 15-inch 14-count ivory Royal Classic napkin

Floss

Cotton embroidery floss in colors listed in key on page 74

Supplies

Needle

Embroidery hoop

INSTRUCTIONS

Tape or zigzag the edges of the napkin to prevent them from fraying. Measure 1 1/2 inches from bottom right side fringe and 2 inches from bottom fringe on one corner of the napkin; begin working the top stitch of the holly leaf there.

Use three plies of floss to work all the cross-stitches. Work all French knots and backstitches using one ply of floss. Press the finished stitchery from the back.

HOLLY TOWEL stitch count:
24 high x 121 wide
HOLLY TOWEL finished design sizes:
14-count fabric – 1 3/4 x 8 5/8 inches
11-count fabric – 2 1/8 x 11 inches
18-count fabric – 1 1/3 x 6 3/4 inches

HOLLY NAPKIN stitch count:
24 high x 30 wide
HOLLY NAPKIN finished design sizes:
14-count fabric – 1 3/4 x 2 1/8 inches
11-count fabric – 2 1/8 x 2 3/4 inches
18-count fabric – 1 1/3 x 1 5/8 inches

ANCHOR	DMC	
◀	9046	321 Christmas red
✕	226	702 Christmas green
▷	256	704 Chartreuse
I	259	772 Loden
●	218	890 Pistachio
○	035	891 Carnation

BACKSTITCH

	310	434 Chestnut– berry stems (1X)
	045	814 Garnet– berries (1X)
	218	890 Pistachio– leaves and stems (1X)

FRENCH KNOT

●	382	3371 Black brown–berries (1X)

HOLLY TOWEL

HOLLY NAPKIN

★★★ CHRISTMAS JAR TOPPERS

As shown on page 68.

MATERIALS *for each jar topper*

Fabrics
6x6-inch piece of 14-count white Aida cloth
1/3 yard of 45-inch-wide red-and-green calico fabric
5-inch-diameter circle of lightweight fusible interfacing

Threads
Cotton embroidery floss in colors listed in key on page 75
Metallic embroidery thread in colors listed in key on page 75

Supplies
Needle
Embroidery hoop
White sewing thread
10-inch piece of 1/16-inch-diameter elastic cord
20-inch piece of 1/4-inch-wide red satin ribbon

INSTRUCTIONS

Tape or zigzag the edges of fabric to prevent fraying. Find center of chart and center of fabric; begin stitching there. Use three plies of floss to work cross-stitches. Work backstitches using one ply of floss or two strands of metallic thread unless otherwise specified.

Fuse interfacing to back of Aida following manufacturer's instructions. Centering the design, cut the Aida into a 4-inch-diameter circle.

From the red-and-green fabric, cut a 37x3 1/8-inch bias strip. With the right sides together, sew the short ends of the strip to form a continuous circle.

Sew a 1/8-inch hem in one long edge of the strip. Run gathering threads 3/8 inch and 1/4 inch from the other long edge of the strip. On wrong side of fabric, machine zigzag stitch over the elastic cord 1 inch from the hemmed edge.

Gather the ruffle to fit the perimeter of the Aida circle. With the right sides together, baste ruffle to the Aida. Adjust the gathers and stitch. Tighten elastic to fit jar. Secure the free end of the elastic. Slip topper over jar. Tie ribbon around topper; knot ribbon ends.

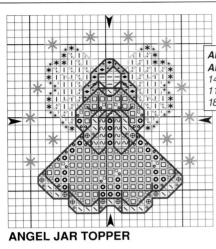

ANGEL stitch count: 25 high x 23 wide
ANGEL finished design sizes:
14-count fabric – 1⁷⁄₈ x 1⁵⁄₈ inches
11-count fabric – 2¹⁄₄ x 2 inches
18-count fabric – 1³⁄₈ x 1¹⁄₄ inches

ANGEL JAR TOPPER

SANTA stitch count: 27 high x 26 wide
SANTA finished design sizes:
14-count fabric – 2 x 1⁷⁄₈ inches
11-count fabric – 2¹⁄₂ x 2³⁄₈ inches
18-count fabric – 1¹⁄₂ x 1¹⁄₂ inches

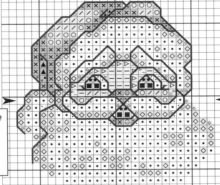

SANTA JAR TOPPER

BELLS stitch count: 22 high x 23 wide
BELLS finished design sizes:
14-count fabric – 1⁵⁄₈ x 1⁵⁄₈ inches
11-count fabric – 2 x 2 inches
18-count fabric – 1¹⁄₄ x 1¹⁄₄ inches

BELL JAR TOPPER

ANCHOR		DMC	
002	•	000	White
110	◎	208	Lavender
1049	◆	301	Mahogany
9046	✕	321	Christmas red
096	□	554	Violet
900	◇	648	Beaver gray
227	●	701	Christmas green
256	+	704	Chartreuse
305	▽	725	True topaz
295	╲	726	Light topaz
890	～	729	Old gold
882	▷	758	Terra cotta
310	★	780	Deep topaz
308	◲	782	Medium topaz
307	⊙	783	Christmas gold
1005	▲	816	Garnet
035	◈	891	Carnation

ANCHOR		DMC	
881	━	945	Ivory
298	⊕	972	Canary
292	Ⅰ	3078	Lemon
382	■	3371	Black brown
033	◯	3706	Medium watermelon
031	╱	3708	Light watermelon
	✳		Kreinik gold #5 Japan

STRAIGHT STITCH
002	╱	000	White – Santa's lip (2X)

BACKSTITCH
	╱		Kreinik gold #5 Japan – wings (1X)
	╱		Kreinik silver #5 Japan – snowflakes (2X)
382	╱	3371	Black brown – all remaining stitches (1X)

FRENCH KNOT
002	•	000	White – bell bow and Santa eyes and nose (1X)

JINGLE BELL PLACE MAT AND NAPKIN

As shown on page 69, place mat is 16x24 inches; napkin is 16x16 inches.

★★★ **JINGLE BELL PLACE MAT**

MATERIALS *for each place mat*

Fabric
14³⁄₄ x 22¹⁄₂-inch piece of 28-count red Jubilee fabric

Threads
Cotton embroidery floss and blending filament in colors listed in key on page 76

Supplies
Needle; embroidery hoop
2¹⁄₄ yards of 1¹⁄₄-inch-wide pre-gathered metallic silver lace
2 yards metallic silver Ribbonfloss braided ribbon
Metallic silver sewing thread

INSTRUCTIONS

Zigzag or serge edges of fabric to prevent fraying. At one corner of place mat, measure 2¹⁄₄ inches from right edge and 1³⁄₈ inches from the bottom; begin stitching bottom row of jingle bell there. Use three plies of floss to work cross-stitches over two threads of fabric. Work blended needle as specified in key. Work backstitches using one ply.

Fold zigzagged edges under ¹⁄₄ inch, mitering corners; topstitch. Sew lace to wrong side of hem, mitering lace at corners. Position braided ribbon over stitching. Zigzag over braided ribbon using metallic silver sewing thread.

★★★ **JINGLE BELL NAPKIN**

MATERIALS *for each napkin*

Fabric
15 x 15-inch piece of 28-count red Jubilee fabric

Threads
Cotton embroidery floss and blending filament in colors listed in key on page 76

Supplies
Needle
Embroidery hoop
¹⁄₈ yard of 1¹⁄₄-inch-wide pre-gathered metallic silver lace
1³⁄₄ yard metallic silver Ribbonfloss braided ribbon
Metallic silver sewing thread

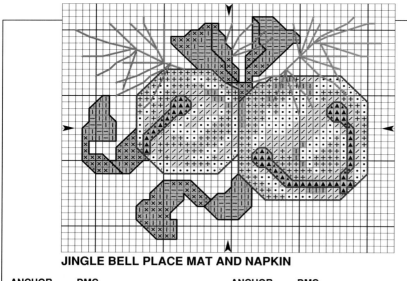

JINGLE BELL PLACE MAT AND NAPKIN

ANCHOR		DMC
401	▲	413 Pewter
046	I	666 Red
043	X	815 Garnet
035	—	3705 Watermelon
BLENDED NEEDLE		
002	•	000 White (2X) and 032 Kreinik pearl blending filament (1X)
235	+	414 Steel (2X) and 034 Kreinik confetti blending filament (1X)
398	∕	415 Pearl gray (2X) and 041 Kreinik confetti pink blending filament (1X)

ANCHOR		DMC
BACKSTITCH		
401	∕	413 Pewter – bells
230	∕	909 Emerald – pine branches
382	∕	3371 Black brown – bow
STRAIGHT STITCH		
230	∕	909 Emerald – pine branches

Stitch count: 34 high x 43 wide
Finished design sizes:
14-count fabric – 2⅜ x 3 inches
11-count fabric – 3 x 4 inches
16-count fabric – 2⅛ x 2⅝ inches

INSTRUCTIONS

Zigzag or serge edges of fabric to prevent fraying. At one corner of napkin, measure 1¾ inches from left side and ⅞ inch from bottom edge; begin stitching bottom row of ribbon end there. Use three plies of floss to work cross-stitches over two threads of fabric. Work blended needle as specified in key. Work backstitches using one ply of floss.

Fold zigzagged edges under ¼ inch, mitering corners, and top-stitch. Sew lace to wrong side of stitched hem, mitering lace at corners. Position braided ribbon over stitching. Zigzag over braided ribbon using silver sewing thread.

★ SLEIGH PARTY FAVOR

As shown on page 69, sleigh is 2 inches tall and 3¼ inches long.
MATERIALS *for each sleigh*
Fabrics
Two 3x4½-inch pieces of 14-count white perforated plastic
3x6-inch piece of 14-count white perforated plastic

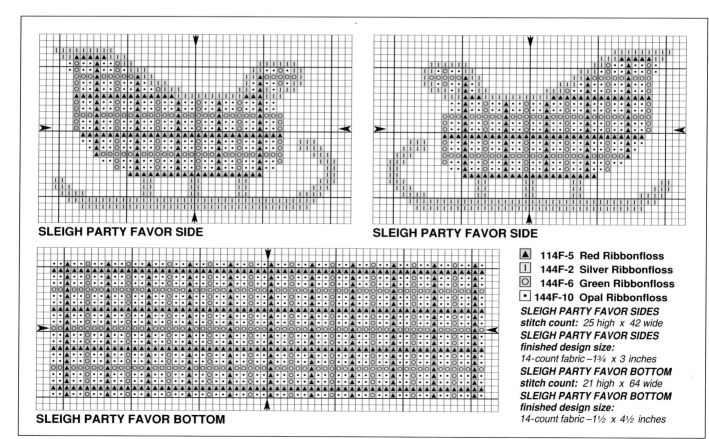

SLEIGH PARTY FAVOR SIDE

SLEIGH PARTY FAVOR SIDE

SLEIGH PARTY FAVOR BOTTOM

▲	114F-5 Red Ribbonfloss
I	144F-2 Silver Ribbonfloss
O	144F-6 Green Ribbonfloss
•	144F-10 Opal Ribbonfloss

SLEIGH PARTY FAVOR SIDES
stitch count: 25 high x 42 wide
SLEIGH PARTY FAVOR SIDES
finished design size:
14-count fabric –1¾ x 3 inches
SLEIGH PARTY FAVOR BOTTOM
stitch count: 21 high x 64 wide
SLEIGH PARTY FAVOR BOTTOM
finished design size:
14-count fabric –1½ x 4½ inches

Thread

Ribbonfloss braided ribbon in colors
   listed in key on page 76

Supplies

Needle

INSTRUCTIONS

Find the center of the desired
chart and the center of one piece of
the plastic; begin stitching there. Use
one strand of the Ribbonfloss braided ribbon to work all of the cross-
stitches. Stitch the remaining charts
in same manner.

Trim each piece of the perforated
plastic one square beyond the
stitched area of the design. Use one
strand of the opal Ribbonfloss
braided ribbon to whipstitch the
sleigh bottom to the sides. Overcast
the top edges of the sleigh using one
strand of the silver Ribbonfloss
braided ribbon.

★ SNOWMAN PLACE CARDS

*As shown on page 69, place cards
are 1½ x 3¾ inches.*

MATERIALS *for each place card*

Fabrics

2x4-inch piece of 14-count red
   perforated paper

3x2-inch piece of 14-count white
   perforated paper

3x2-inch piece of white card stock

3x3¾-inch piece of red card stock

¼x3-inch piece of green and white
   fabric

Floss

Cotton embroidery floss in colors
   listed in key

Supplies

Tracing paper; graph paper

Needle

Eight black seed beads

Three orange seed beads

Three ⅛-inch-diameter black buttons

Nine 1½-millimeter pearls

Crafts glue

INSTRUCTIONS

Transfer snowman shape onto
tracing paper. Trace around shape
onto white perforated paper. Attach
beads and buttons using one ply of
black floss. Thread a needle with two
plies of orange floss. Bring needle up
from the back at the top marked

position. Thread the orange beads on
the needle; return thread to the back
at bottom marked position, and
secure. Glue the perforated snowman to the white card stock; let dry.
Cut out along the marked outline.
Tie fabric around the snowman's
neck; set aside.

Chart desired name, separating
letters with one square. Measure
¼ inch from top edge and ¼ inch
from left edge of red perforated

paper; begin stitching top corner of
border there. Work backstitches and
straight stitches using three plies.
Attach pearls using two plies of white
(DMC 000) floss. Cut out one square
beyond the stitching as indicated on
the chart.

Fold the card stock in half to form
a 1½x3¾-inch rectangle. Glue the
red perforated paper to one side of
the card stock. Glue the snowman to
the right side of the place card.

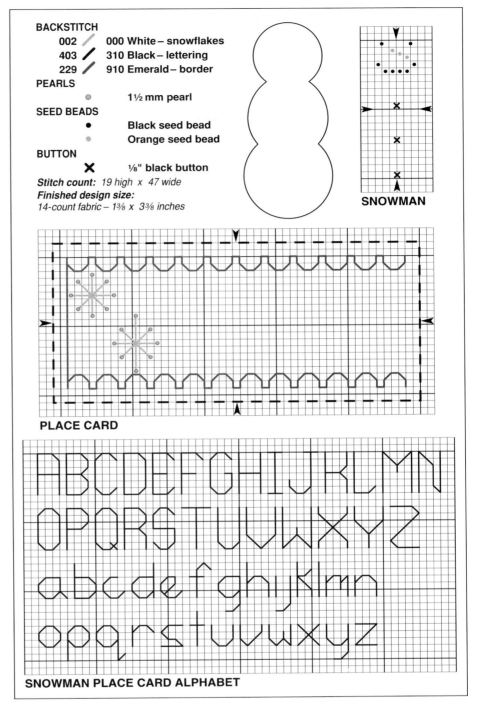

BACKSTITCH

002 ╱ 000 White – snowflakes

403 ╱ 310 Black – lettering

229 ╱ 910 Emerald – border

PEARLS

● 1½ mm pearl

SEED BEADS

● Black seed bead

● Orange seed bead

BUTTON

✕ ⅛" black button

Stitch count: 19 high x 47 wide

Finished design size:
14-count fabric – 1⅜ x 3⅜ inches

SNOWMAN

PLACE CARD

SNOWMAN PLACE CARD ALPHABET

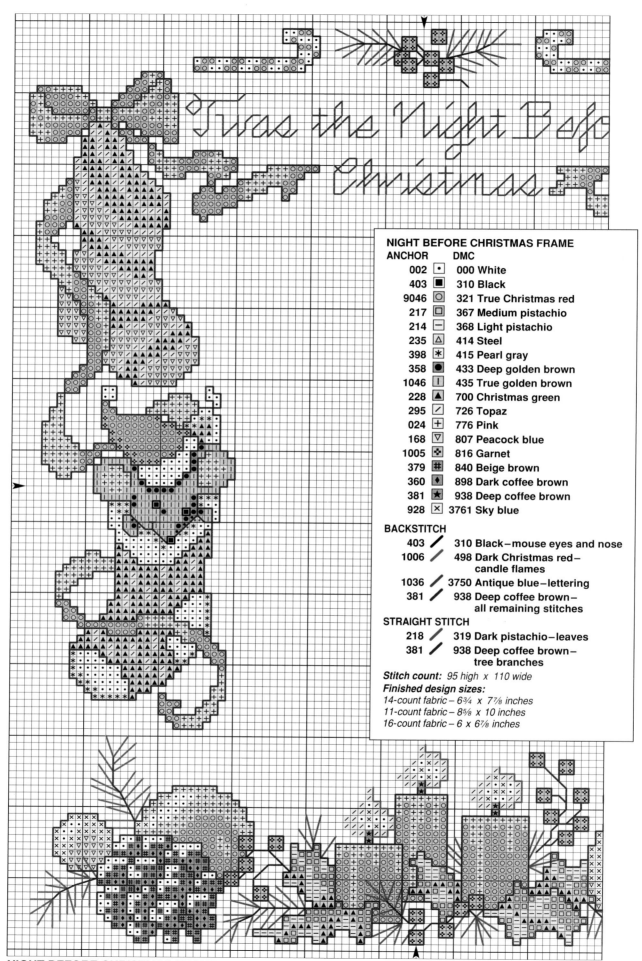

'Twas the Night Before Christmas

NIGHT BEFORE CHRISTMAS FRAME

ANCHOR		DMC	
002	•	000	White
403	■	310	Black
9046	◎	321	True Christmas red
217	▫	367	Medium pistachio
214	−	368	Light pistachio
235	△	414	Steel
398	✳	415	Pearl gray
358	●	433	Deep golden brown
1046			435	True golden brown
228	▲	700	Christmas green
295	╱	726	Topaz
024	+	776	Pink
168	▽	807	Peacock blue
1005	✤	816	Garnet
379	▦	840	Beige brown
360	◆	898	Dark coffee brown
381	★	938	Deep coffee brown
928	⊠	3761	Sky blue

BACKSTITCH

403	╱	310	Black—mouse eyes and nose
1006	╱	498	Dark Christmas red—candle flames
1036	╱	3750	Antique blue—lettering
381	╱	938	Deep coffee brown—all remaining stitches

STRAIGHT STITCH

218	╱	319	Dark pistachio—leaves
381	╱	938	Deep coffee brown—tree branches

Stitch count: 95 high x 110 wide
Finished design sizes:
14-count fabric – 6¾ x 7⅞ inches
11-count fabric – 8⅝ x 10 inches
16-count fabric – 6 x 6⅞ inches

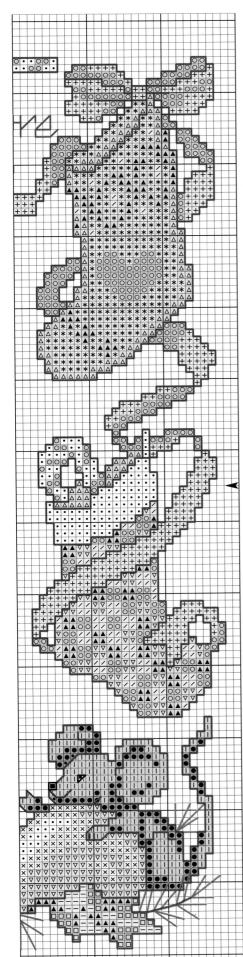

★★★ NIGHT BEFORE CHRISTMAS FRAME

As shown on page 70.

MATERIALS

Fabric
Two 12½ x 11-inch pieces of 14-count white Aida cloth

Floss
Cotton embroidery floss in colors listed in key on page 78

Supplies
Needle; embroidery hoop
White sewing thread
9½ x 8¼-inch self-stick mounting board with foam
Crafts knife; crafts glue
9½ x 8¼-inch piece of lightweight cardboard

INSTRUCTIONS

Tape or zigzag edges of fabric. Find center of chart and one piece of Aida; begin stitching there. Use three plies to work cross-stitches. Work backstitches and straight stitches using one ply. Work basting stitches ¼ inch in from stitching on all sides. Cut a 4¾-inch-high and 3¼-inch-wide rectangle in center of mounting board with crafts knife. Sew Aida pieces together, right sides facing, along basting lines. Cut out center rectangle, clip corners, and turn right side out. Press. Position stitchery over mounting board, turn edges to back. Attach purchased frame stand.

★★★ SANTA ORNAMENT

As shown on page 70, Santa is 6½ inches tall.

MATERIALS

Fabrics
9 x 12-inch piece of 11-count Victorian red Aida cloth
9 x 12-inch piece of Christmas print fabric

Threads
Cotton embroidery floss in colors listed in key on page 80
#8 gold braid

Supplies
Needle; embroidery hoop
Red sewing thread
16-inch piece of ¼-inch-wide red-and-gold braid
½ yard of ⅛-inch-diameter white-and-gold cord

¾-inch-diameter white pom pom
1¾-inch-tall gold bell with clapper
Two copper seed beads
58 gold seed beads
Crafts glue

INSTRUCTIONS

Tape or zigzag the edges of Aida cloth to prevent fraying. Find center of the chart and the center of fabric; begin stitching there. Use three plies of floss to work cross-stitches. Work French knots using one ply of floss. Work backstitches using two plies. Use two plies of matching floss to sew copper seed beads to the center of each eye and a Victorian gold seed bead to each metallic gold star burst on Santa's coat.

Cut out the Santa ¼ inch beyond the stitched area of the design as indicated on chart. Use Aida as a pattern to cut out a matching lining from the Christmas print fabric. Turn the straight edges of both the Santa and the lining fabric under ¼ inch. With the wrong sides together, and the bottom raw edges even, glue the lining to the Aida along the turned under straight edges. Turn the curved bottom raw edges ¼ inch to inside; stitch.

Tie the white-and-gold cord ends to the top of the bell. Wrap the Santa into a cone shape with the bell inside near the top and the cord loop coming out the point. Slipstitch the side edges together to form the cone. Glue the red-and-gold braid around the bottom. Glue pom pom to the stitched ball on Santa's hat.

★★★ TREE ORNAMENT

As shown on page 70, tree is 7 inches tall.

MATERIALS

Fabrics
9 x 12-inch piece of 11-count green Aida cloth
9 x 12-inch piece of Christmas print fabric
3 x 3-inch piece of 11-count white Aida cloth
2½ x 2½-inch piece of white felt

Threads
Cotton embroidery floss in colors listed in key on page 81
Novelty thread in color listed in key on page 81

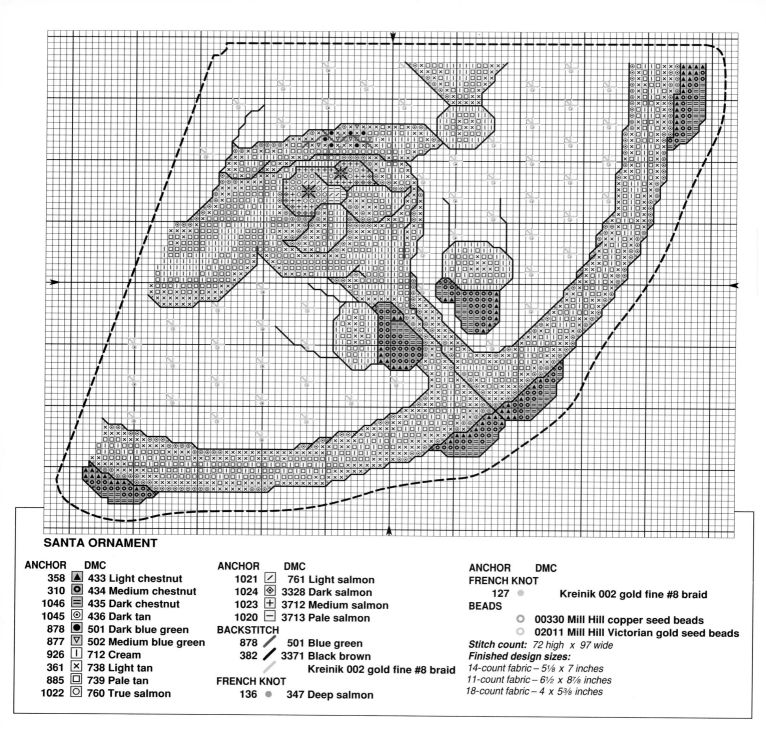

SANTA ORNAMENT

ANCHOR		DMC		ANCHOR		DMC	
358	▲	433 Light chestnut		1021	╱	761 Light salmon	
310	⊙	434 Medium chestnut		1024	◈	3328 Dark salmon	
1046	⊟	435 Dark chestnut		1023	+	3712 Medium salmon	
1045	⊙	436 Dark tan		1020	−	3713 Pale salmon	
878	●	501 Dark blue green		**BACKSTITCH**			
877	▽	502 Medium blue green		878	╱	501 Blue green	
926	‖	712 Cream		382	╱	3371 Black brown	
361	✕	738 Light tan			╱	Kreinik 002 gold fine #8 braid	
885	▢	739 Pale tan		**FRENCH KNOT**			
1022	⊘	760 True salmon		136	●	347 Deep salmon	

ANCHOR		DMC	
FRENCH KNOT			
127	●	Kreinik 002 gold fine #8 braid	
BEADS			
	○	00330 Mill Hill copper seed beads	
	○	02011 Mill Hill Victorian gold seed beads	

Stitch count: 72 high x 97 wide
Finished design sizes:
14-count fabric – 5⅛ x 7 inches
11-count fabric – 6½ x 8⅞ inches
18-count fabric – 4 x 5⅜ inches

Supplies
Needle
Embroidery hoop
Green and white sewing threads
16 inches of ¼-inch-wide
   red-and-gold braid
½ yard of ⅛-inch-diameter
   white-and-gold cord
1¾-inch-tall gold bell with clapper
Eleven red sequins
Ten gold sequins
Polyester fiberfill
Crafts glue

INSTRUCTIONS
Tape or zigzag edges of Aida pieces to prevent fraying. For both star and tree, find center of desired chart and center of the appropriate fabric; begin stitching there. Use two plies of floss to work cross-stitches. Work backstitches and French knots using one ply of floss or one strand of the novelty thread.

Cut out tree ¼ inch beyond stitched area of design as indicated on chart. Use Aida as a pattern to cut a matching lining from Christmas print fabric. Turn straight edges of both tree and lining fabric under ¼ inch. With wrong sides together and bottom raw edges even, glue the lining to Aida along turned under straight edges. Turn curved bottom raw edges ¼ inch to inside; stitch.

Tie white-and-gold cord ends to top of bell. Wrap tree into a cone shape with bell inside near top and cord loop coming out the point. Slipstitch side edges together to

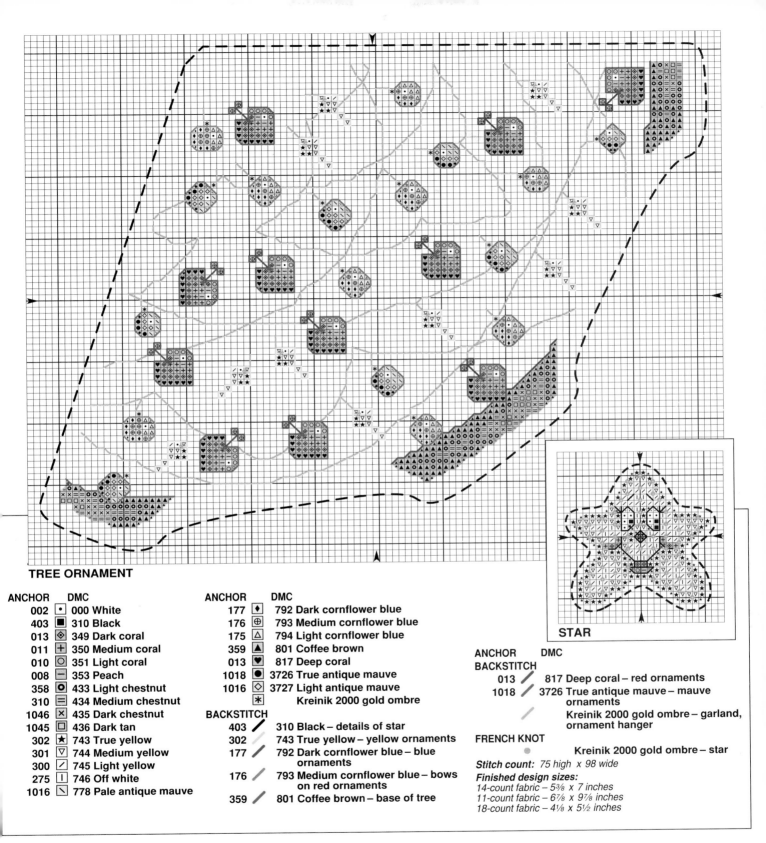

TREE ORNAMENT

ANCHOR		DMC
002	·	000 White
403	■	310 Black
013	◇	349 Dark coral
011	+	350 Medium coral
010	○	351 Light coral
008	−	353 Peach
358	◉	433 Light chestnut
310	=	434 Medium chestnut
1046	×	435 Dark chestnut
1045	□	436 Dark tan
302	★	743 True yellow
301	▽	744 Medium yellow
300	∕	745 Light yellow
275	I	746 Off white
1016	◣	778 Pale antique mauve

ANCHOR		DMC
177	◆	792 Dark cornflower blue
176	⊕	793 Medium cornflower blue
175	△	794 Light cornflower blue
359	▲	801 Coffee brown
013	❤	817 Deep coral
1018	●	3726 True antique mauve
1016	◇	3727 Light antique mauve
	✳	Kreinik 2000 gold ombre

BACKSTITCH

ANCHOR		DMC
403	╱	310 Black – details of star
302	╱	743 True yellow – yellow ornaments
177	╱	792 Dark cornflower blue – blue ornaments
176	╱	793 Medium cornflower blue – bows on red ornaments
359	╱	801 Coffee brown – base of tree

STAR

ANCHOR		DMC
BACKSTITCH		
013	╱	817 Deep coral – red ornaments
1018	╱	3726 True antique mauve – mauve ornaments
	╱	Kreinik 2000 gold ombre – garland, ornament hanger

FRENCH KNOT

	●	Kreinik 2000 gold ombre – star

Stitch count: 75 high x 98 wide
Finished design sizes:
14-count fabric – 5⅜ x 7 inches
11-count fabric – 6⅞ x 9⅞ inches
18-count fabric – 4⅛ x 5½ inches

form cone. Glue red-and-gold braid around bottom. Glue red sequin to each red ornament on tree and gold sequin to each yellow ornament.

Cut out star ¼-inch beyond the stitched area of design as indicated on chart. Use star as a pattern to cut a matching back from felt. With the wrong sides together, whipstitch shapes together leaving an opening at bottom. Cut a ¼-inch-long slit across back of the star near top.

Thread the cord loop through bottom of star and out the slit. Lightly stuff star and position it on the point of the tree. Whipstitch star to tree around the bottom opening of the star.

ANGELIC DELIGHTS

*A*s traditional bearers of good news, angels come in all shapes and sizes. Our heavenly cross-stitched angels will bring messages of glad tidings into your holiday home.

Add a brilliant accent to Christmas packages by adorning them with this heavenly ribbon created by repeating the simple angel motif on 28-count white linen. The complete instructions and chart are on page 86.

Designer: Barbara Sestok
Photographer: Scott Little

Little Angel Stocking

Stitch this adorable stocking on 25-count bone Lugana fabric as a gift for a special little girl. She will truly treasure this sweet angel as a bearer of Christmas goodies. The complete instructions and chart begin on page 86.

Designer: Barbara Sestok
Photographer: Scott Little

Glad Tidings Sampler

Cross-stitch our trumpeting and rejoicing angels as a celebration of the holiday season. Twinkling stars made from metallic threads and specialty stitches enhance the glorious design. Stitched on 28-count ivory Jobelan fabric, the sampler makes a special gift. Complete instructions and chart are on pages 88–91.

Designer: Mary B. Jones ◆ Photographer: Scott Little

Heavenly Choir Sampler

This jewel-colored angel choir is singing praise for the approaching Christmas season. Stitch this celestial piece on 36-count tea Irish linen and create a graceful addition to your holiday decorating. The complete instructions and chart begin on page 90.

Designer: Patricia Andrle
Photographer: Hopkins Associates

Sweetness and Lace Angel

Bless your home with this heavenly angel created with 14-count perforated plastic, flat white lace, and tulle. Metallic threads add sparkle to her wings and dress as she sits atop the Christmas tree or amongst a favorite holiday centerpiece. The complete instructions and chart are on page 91.

Designer: Carole Rodgers
Photographer: Hopkins Associates

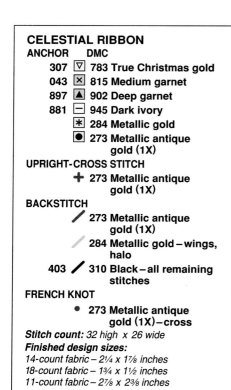

CELESTIAL RIBBON

ANCHOR		DMC	
307	▽	783	True Christmas gold
043	☒	815	Medium garnet
897	▲	902	Deep garnet
881	⊟	945	Dark ivory
	✳	284	Metallic gold
	●	273	Metallic antique gold (1X)

UPRIGHT-CROSS STITCH
	✚	273	Metallic antique gold (1X)

BACKSTITCH
	╱	273	Metallic antique gold (1X)
	╱	284	Metallic gold – wings, halo
403	╱	310	Black – all remaining stitches

FRENCH KNOT
	●	273	Metallic antique gold (1X) – cross

Stitch count: 32 high x 26 wide
Finished design sizes:
14-count fabric – 2¼ x 1⅞ inches
18-count fabric – 1¾ x 1½ inches
11-count fabric – 2⅞ x 2⅜ inches

★★★ CELESTIAL RIBBON

As shown on page 82, finished ribbon is 2 inches wide.

MATERIALS
Fabrics
5-inch-wide piece of 28-count white linen in desired length
1½-inch-wide piece of lightweight fusible interfacing in desired length
Threads
Cotton embroidery floss and metallic thread in colors listed in key
Supplies
Needle; embroidery hoop

INSTRUCTIONS
Tape or zigzag edges of fabric. Find vertical center of chart and vertical center of fabric. Measure 1 inch from one end of linen strip; begin stitching there. Use three plies of floss or one strand of metallic thread to work cross-stitches over two threads of fabric. Work upright-cross stitches and French knots using one strand of thread. Work backstitches using one ply of floss or one strand of thread. Continue stitching pattern until desired length is reached. Centering design, trim 3 inches wide. Trim short ends 1 inch from stitching.

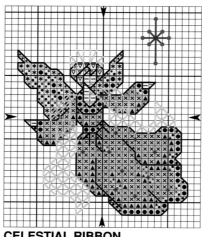

CELESTIAL RIBBON

Press edges under ½ inch on all sides. Center interfacing on back of stitchery with interfacing over the pressed edges of linen strip. Fuse following manufacturer's instructions.

★★★★ LITTLE ANGEL STOCKING

As shown on page 83, stocking is 13 inches tall.

MATERIALS
Fabrics
18 x 13-inch piece of 25-count bone Lugana fabric
¼ yard of fusible fleece
1⅓ yards of 45-inch-wide red and white pin dot fabric
Threads
Cotton embroidery floss and #8 braid in colors listed in key on page 87
One additional skein *each* of Christmas red (DMC 321), and off white (DMC 746)
Supplies
Needle; tapestry needle
Embroidery hoop
1 yard of ⅛-inch-wide red satin ribbon; sewing thread
1¼ yards of ⅛-inch-diameter cording
Ten ⅜-inch-diameter gold jingle bells
2¼ yards *each* of 1/16-inch-wide cream and wine ribbon
Twelve ⅝-inch-diameter gold jingle bells; four ⅞-inch-diameter snowflake charms

INSTRUCTIONS
Tape or zigzag edges of Lugana fabric to prevent fraying. Find center of chart and fabric; begin stitching

there. Use three plies of floss to work cross-stitches over two threads of fabric. Work straight stitches and French knots as specified in key. Work running stitches using one strand of braid. Work backstitches using one ply. Attach beads using one ply.

For braid, join four plies *each* of topaz (DMC 725) and Christmas gold (DMC 783). Fold in half and tack looped end at bottom of hairline near side of face. Refer to the photograph on page 83 for placement. Separate plies into three sections; braid. Tie a 5-inch length of ⅛-inch-wide ribbon around end of braid. Repeat for opposite side of head. Trim floss and ribbon ends.

Thread a tapestry needle with an 8-inch piece of ⅛-inch-wide ribbon. Working from front of fabric, insert needle at one side of angel's waist. Bring ribbon across back of angel to opposite side of waist; bring needle back through fabric to front. Tie ribbon into bow at center of waist. Tack ribbon knot to secure; trim ends.

Thread remaining ⅛-inch-wide ribbon into the tapestry needle. Beginning at one hand, insert needle through fabric as before. Bring the ribbon across back of hand, up and across skirt front, down fabric and across back of opposite hand, and then up to front of fabric. Thread a needle with red floss. Twisting ribbon as desired, tack ribbon to fabric at intervals. Attach bells with sewing thread. Trim ribbon ends.

Use marker to draw a line ¼ inch beyond outline of stocking. Fuse fleece to back of Lugana following manufacturer's instructions. Cut out stocking ¼ inch beyond marker line. Use fabric stocking as a pattern to cut one back and two lining pieces from cotton fabric. Also cut a 2¼ x 4½-inch hanging strip, a 4¼ x 26-inch bias ruffle strip, a 1⅛ x 30-inch piping strip, a 1⅛ x 14-inch bias piping strip, a 5½ x 28-inch bias bow, a 5½ x 13-inch bias strip for bow, and a 1½ x 3¾-inch bow center from the cotton fabric. All measurements include a ¼-inch seam allowance.

Cut a 30-inch length of cording; center lengthwise on wrong side of

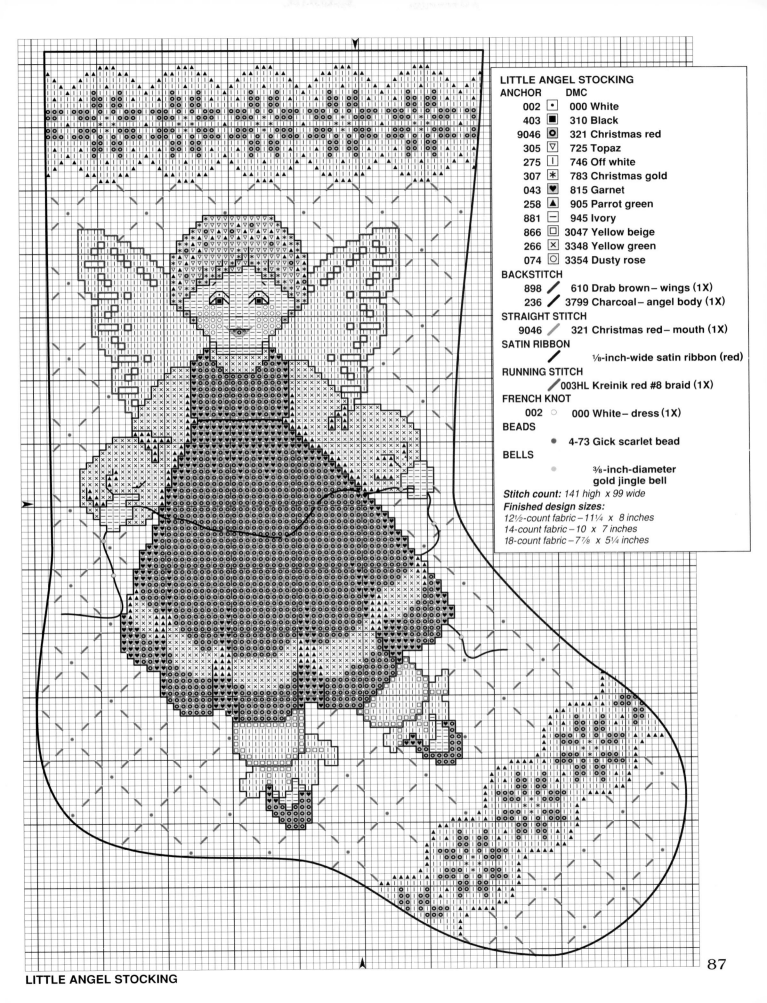

LITTLE ANGEL STOCKING

ANCHOR		DMC	
002	⬒	000	White
403	⬛	310	Black
9046	◉	321	Christmas red
305	▽	725	Topaz
275			746	Off white
307	✳	783	Christmas gold
043	♥	815	Garnet
258	▲	905	Parrot green
881	−	945	Ivory
866	▢	3047	Yellow beige
266	✕	3348	Yellow green
074	◯	3354	Dusty rose

BACKSTITCH

898	╱	610	Drab brown – wings (1X)
236	╱	3799	Charcoal – angel body (1X)

STRAIGHT STITCH

9046	╱	321	Christmas red – mouth (1X)

SATIN RIBBON

╱	⅛-inch-wide satin ribbon (red)

RUNNING STITCH

╱	003HL Kreinik red #8 braid (1X)

FRENCH KNOT

002	◦	000	White – dress (1X)

BEADS

●	4-73 Gick scarlet bead

BELLS

●	⅜-inch-diameter gold jingle bell

Stitch count: 141 high x 99 wide
Finished design sizes:
12½-count fabric – 11¼ x 8 inches
14-count fabric – 10 x 7 inches
18-count fabric – 7⅞ x 5¼ inches

LITTLE ANGEL STOCKING

87

30-inch piping strip. Fold fabric around cording bringing raw edges together. Use a zipper foot to sew through both fabric layers close to cording. Pin covered cording around sides and foot of stocking front with raw edges even; baste. Construct top piping in same manner, using remaining cording and 14-inch piping strip. Sew front to back, right sides together along basting lines. Leave top edge open. Baste cording around top of stocking with raw edges even.

Press long edges of hanging strip under ¼ inch. Fold strip in half lengthwise; topstitch. Fold in half to form a loop; tack inside top left edge of stocking.

Sew short ends of ruffle strip together to form a continuous circle. Fold in half lengthwise; press. Sew a gathering thread through both layers of ruffle ¼ inch from raw edges. Pull threads to fit perimeter of stocking top with raw edges even; adjust gathers evenly. Sew ruffle to stocking top along piping stitching line.

Sew lining pieces together, right sides together, leaving top open and opening at bottom of foot; *do not* turn. Stitch stocking to lining at top edges with right sides together; turn. Slip-stitch opening closed. Tuck lining into stocking; press carefully.

For bow, fold 28-inch bias strip in half lengthwise, right sides together. Taper ends to a point; stitch, leaving opening in center. Turn and press. Fold in half crosswise; sew across all layers, 6½ inches from folded edge. Bring folded edge to stitching line and stitch again. Gather fabric at stitching line; hand sew to secure. For bow center, fold remaining fabric in thirds lengthwise, with wrong sides

together; turn under ¼ inch on back raw edge and stitch. Wrap around center of bow; stitch.

Cut an 11-inch piece from each ¹⁄₁₆-inch ribbon. Sew a bell on each end of ribbons. Sew two more bells to each ribbon at 1 inch intervals. Join ends of remaining ribbons; tie into a bow with three loops on each side. Tack ribbon bow to center of fabric bow. Sew a snowflake to each ribbon end.

Fold remaining bias strip in half lengthwise, right sides together. Stitch, leaving ends open; turn and press. Overlap ends to make a loop; stitch. Gather center of loop. Position fabric loop over center of bow and stitch to secure. Sew finished bow to upper left edge of stocking.

★★★★ GLAD TIDINGS SAMPLER

As shown on page 84.

MATERIALS
Fabric
18x14-inch piece of 28-count ivory Jobelan fabric

Threads
Cotton embroidery floss and blending filament as listed in key

Supplies
Needle; embroidery hoop
Graph paper; pencil
Desired frame and mat

INSTRUCTIONS
Tape or zigzag edges of fabric to prevent fraying. Find the center of chart and center of the fabric; begin stitching there.

Use three plies of floss to work cross-stitches over two threads of fabric. Work the blended needle as specified in key.

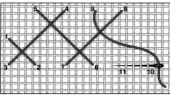

Step 1

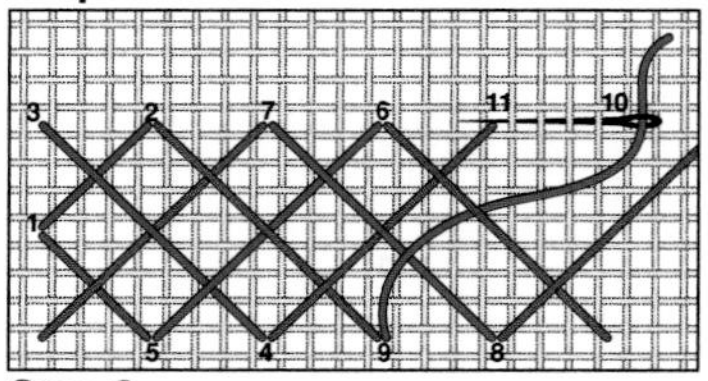

Step 2
Interlaced Double Herringbone

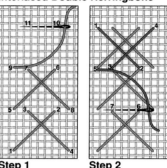

Step 1
Vertical Modified Bazaar Stitch   **Step 2**

Star Stitch

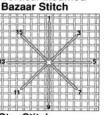

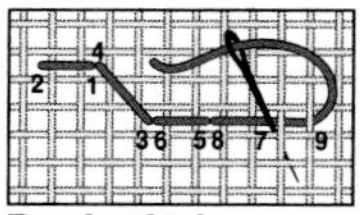

Backstitch

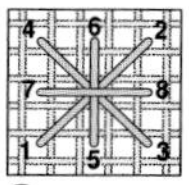

Smyrna Cross Stitch

For each section of the design, work all cross-stitches before working specialty stitches. Referring to the diagrams, *above,* work Smyrna cross stitches, star stitches, interlaced double herringbone stitches, and vertical modified bazaar stitch, as specified in key. Work the straight stitches and the backstitches as specified in key.

GLAD TIDINGS SAMPLER

ANCHOR		DMC	
891	✓	676	Light old gold
890	▢	729	Medium old gold
4146	▬	950	Rose beige
1028	●	3685	Deep mauve
060	◇	3688	Medium mauve
069	⊞	3803	Dark mauve
877	▲	3815	Dark celadon green
876	◉	3816	True celadon green
875	☒	3817	Light celadon green
890	◆	3829	Deep old gold

BLENDED NEEDLE
891	▽	676 Light old gold (2X) and 002HL Kreinik gold blending filament (1X)
890	✳	729 Medium old gold (2X) and 002HL Kreinik gold blending filament (1X)

BACKSTITCH
1028	/	3685 Deep mauve – personalized name and date; saying and lower angel skirt outline
876	/	3816 True celadon green – upper angel skirt outline and design

SMYRNA CROSS STITCH
890	✳	729 Medium old gold (3X)

STAR STITCH
890	✳	729 Medium old gold (2X) and 002HL Kreinik gold blending filament (1X)

BACKSTITCH AND STRAIGHT STITCH
890	✳	3829 Deep old gold (3X)

INTERLACED DOUBLE HERRINGBONE
1028	✕	3685 Deep mauve (3X) and
877	✕	3815 Dark celadon green (3X)

VERTICAL MODIFIED BAZAAR STITCH
877	✕	3815 Dark celadon green (3X) and
876	✕	3816 True celadon green (3X)

Stitch count: 154 high x 100 wide
Finished design sizes:
18-count fabric – 6⅜ x 7½ inches
11-count fabric – 10½ x 12¼ inches
14-count fabric – 8¼ x 9⅝ inches

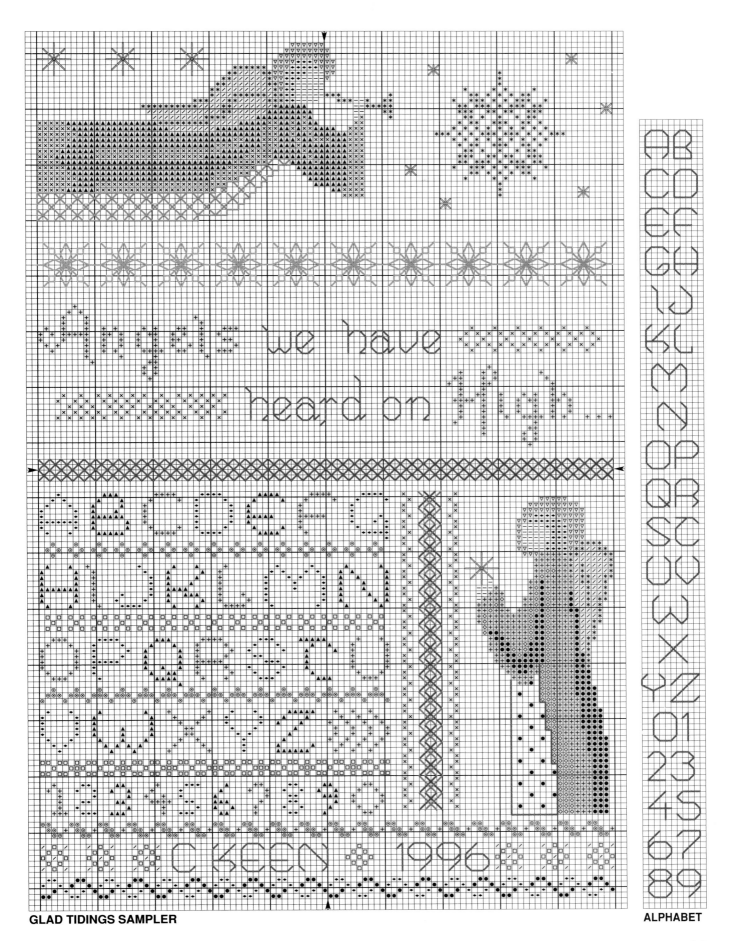

GLAD TIDINGS SAMPLER

ALPHABET

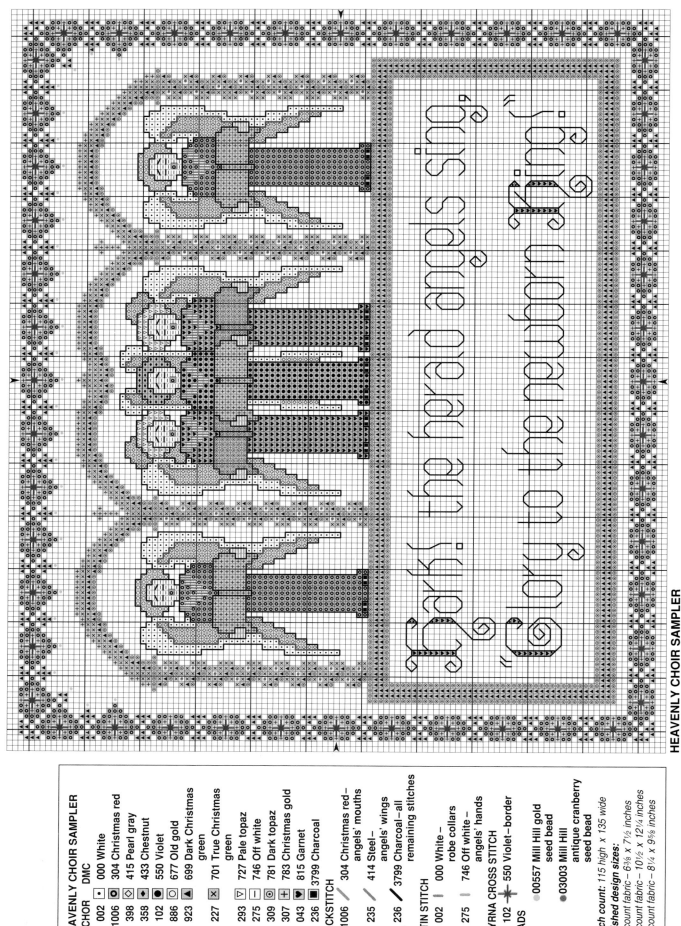

HEAVENLY CHOIR SAMPLER

ANCHOR		DMC	
002	·	000	White
1006	⊙	304	Christmas red
398	◇	415	Pearl gray
358	◆	433	Chestnut
102	●	550	Violet
886	○	677	Old gold
923	◀	699	Dark Christmas green
227	⊠	701	True Christmas green
293	▷	727	Pale topaz
275			746	Off white
309	⊙	781	Dark topaz
307	+	783	Christmas gold
043	▶	815	Garnet
236	■	3799	Charcoal

BACKSTITCH
- 1006 — 304 Christmas red—angels' mouths
- 235 — 414 Steel—angels' wings
- 236 — 3799 Charcoal—all remaining stitches

SATIN STITCH
- 002 — 000 White—robe collars
- 275 — 746 Off white—angels' hands

SMYRNA CROSS STITCH
- 102 ✳ 550 Violet—border

BEADS
- 00557 Mill Hill gold seed bead
- 03003 Mill Hill antique cranberry seed bead

Stitch count: 115 high x 135 wide
Finished design sizes:
18-count fabric—6⅜ x 7½ inches
11-count fabric—10½ x 12¼ inches
14-count fabric—8¼ x 9⅝ inches

HEAVENLY CHOIR SAMPLER

Chart name using alphabet on page 89. Separate letters with one square. For longer names, use initials. Position bottom of name two threads above the bottom border stitches. Press, mat, and frame.

★★★ HEAVENLY CHOIR SAMPLER

As shown on page 85.

MATERIALS

Fabric

11x12-inch piece of 36-count tea Irish linen

Floss

Cotton embroidery floss in colors listed in key on page 90

Supplies

Needle; embroidery hoop
Seed beads in colors listed in key on page 90
Desired frame and mat

INSTRUCTIONS

Tape or zigzag the edges of fabric to prevent fraying. Find center of chart and center of fabric; begin stitching there.

Use three plies of floss to work cross-stitches over two threads of fabric. Work the satin stitches and Smyrna cross stitches as specified in key. Work backstitches using one ply unless otherwise specified in key. Attach beads using one ply matching floss. Press, mat, and frame.

★★ SWEETNESS AND LACE ANGEL

As shown on page 85, angel is 8½ inches tall.

MATERIALS

Fabric

Two 6x8-inch pieces of 14-count clear perforated plastic

Threads

Cotton embroidery floss in colors listed in key
#8 braid in colors listed in key

Supplies

Needle
White sewing thread
22-inch piece of 7½-inch-wide flat white lace
7½ x 56-inch piece of white tulle
Hot-glue gun
Glue sticks

INSTRUCTIONS

Find center of angel front chart and center of one piece of plastic; begin stitching there. Use three plies of floss or one strand of braid to work cross-stitches. Work French knots as specified in key. Work backstitches using one ply. Stitch the angel back chart in the same manner. Trim plastic one square beyond stitching.

Whipstitch front and back together using sewing thread, and leaving bottom edge open. Sew short ends of lace together to form a continuous circle. Work gathering stitches ⅛ inch from edge of lace. Repeat for the tulle.

To form skirt, slip tulle inside lace with the gathered edges even. Insert skirt into bottom opening of angel; glue to secure.

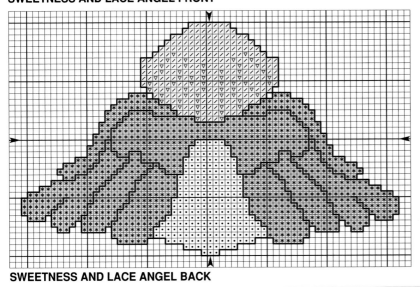

SWEETNESS AND LACE ANGEL FRONT

SWEETNESS AND LACE ANGEL BACK

SWEETNESS AND LACE ANGEL

ANCHOR		DMC	
002	•	000	White
403	■	310	Black
9046	☒	321	Christmas red
1005	▲	498	Dark Christmas red
891	◿	676	Light old gold
890	▽	729	Medium old gold
024	◯	776	Pink
1011	−	948	Peach
140	⊞	3755	Baby blue
	⊕	001C	Kreinik silver #8 fine braid
	✳	002	Kreinik gold #8 fine braid

BACKSTITCH

382	╱	3371 Black brown – all stitches

FRENCH KNOT

002	●	000 White – eyes (1X)

SWEETNESS AND LACE ANGEL FRONT stitch count:
40 high x 63 wide
SWEETNESS AND LACE ANGEL FRONT finished design sizes:
14-count fabric – 2⅞ x 4½ inches
8½-count fabric – 4¾ x 7¾ inches
SWEETNESS AND LACE ANGEL BACK stitch count:
40 high x 63 wide
SWEETNESS AND LACE ANGEL BACK finished design sizes:
14-count fabric – 2⅞ x 4½ inches
8½-count fabric – 4¾ x 7¾ inches

TOYS AND GAMES FROM SANTA'S WORKSHOP

Dolls and toys and games
(oh, my), fill Santa's bag
(with a little help from you).
Each project is stitched with love and designed
to be enjoyed by little ones on your list.

Teddy bears and rocking horses parade
up and down 28-count ruby linen so
cleverly finished as ribbon. Complete
instructions and chart for our *Colorful
Toy Ribbon* are on page 97.

Designer: Barbara Sestok
Photographer: Scott Little

92

Sailor Dolls

Stitch and give our sailor dolls—they're sure to become favorite companions for any little seafarer. Worked on 28-count white Jubilee fabric, the pieces have a sew-on backing and are then stuffed with fiberfill. The complete instructions and charts are on pages 98–99.

Designer: Susan Cage-Knoch ◆ Photographer: Hopkins Associates

Paper Dolls

Girls of all ages will enjoy stitching and playing with these clever paper dolls. The designs can be stitched as a grouping on one piece of 14-count perforated paper, or worked separately. Complete instructions and charts are on pages 100–101.

Designer: Carole Rodgers
Photographer: Hopkins Associates

Circus Pull Toys

These three-dimensional brightly-colored pull toys will make great stocking stuffers for any little one in your family. Each animal stitches up quickly on 14-count perforated plastic. Fun-shaped buttons serve as wheels for this playful threesome. Complete instructions and charts begin on page 102.

Designer: Carole Rodgers
Photographer: Hopkins Associates

Candyland Checkers

Handcrafted games are favorites at Christmastime, and our candy motifs make this checkerboard extra sweet! On a cross-stitched game board, red and green squares are surrounded by symbols of the holiday season. Airplanes and horses are ready to serve as playing pieces for a festive match. When finished, store the game in the wooden box. Instructions and charts begin on page 105.

Designer: Virginia Soskin
Photographer: Scott Little

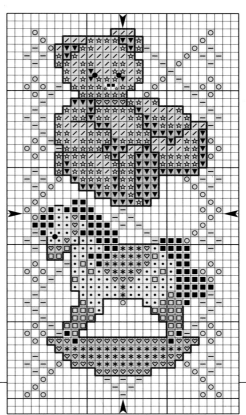

COLORFUL TOY RIBBON

ANCHOR		DMC		ANCHOR	DMC
403	■	310 Black		**BACKSTITCH**	
9046	♡	321 Christmas red		236 ╱	3799 Charcoal—
891	╱	676 Light old gold			all backstitches (1X)
901	☆	680 Dark old gold		**FRENCH KNOTS**	
238	–	703 Chartreuse		403 ●	310 Black—eyes (2X)
132	✳	797 Royal blue			
944	▼	869 Hazel			
1033	▢	932 Antique blue			
246	○	986 Forest green			
1037	•	3756 Baby blue			

Stitch count: 48 high x 25 wide

Finished design sizes:
14-count fabric – 3½ x 1⅞ inches
11-count fabric – 4⅜ x 2⅜ inches
18-count fabric – 2⅔ x 1½ inches

★★ COLORFUL TOY RIBBON

As shown on page 92, finished ribbon is 2 inches wide.

MATERIALS

Fabrics

5-inch-wide piece of 28-count ruby linen in desired length

1½-inch-wide piece of lightweight fusible interfacing in desired length

Floss

Cotton embroidery floss in colors listed in key

Supplies

Needle; embroidery hoop

INSTRUCTIONS

Tape or zigzag edges of fabric to prevent fraying. Find the vertical center of the chart and the vertical center of the fabric. Measure 1 inch from one end of the linen strip; begin stitching there. Use three plies of floss to work cross-stitches over two threads of fabric. Work French knots using two plies. Work the backstitches using one ply of floss. Continue stitching the pattern until the desired length is reached. Centering the design, trim the linen to measure 3 inches wide. Trim the short ends of the linen strip 1 inch from the stitching.

Press edges under ½ inch on all sides of the linen strip. Center the interfacing on back of stitchery with interfacing over pressed edges of linen strip. Fuse following the manufacturer's instructions.

★★★ SAILOR DOLLS

As shown on page 93, dolls are 7 3/8 inches tall.

MATERIALS *for each doll*

Fabric
Two 10 x 7-inch pieces of 28-count white Jubilee fabric

Floss
Cotton embroidery floss in colors listed in key on page 99

Supplies
Needle
Embroidery hoop
White sewing thread
Polyester fiberfill

INSTRUCTIONS

Tape or zigzag the edges of the Jubilee fabric to prevent them from fraying. Find the center of one chart and the center of one piece of fabric; begin stitching there. Use three plies of floss to work cross-stitches over two threads of fabric. Work the backstitches as specified in the key. Press finished stitchery from the back.

Use dotted line on pattern as a guide to draw around figure approximately 3/4 inches from stitching; cut out. Use stitched Jubilee fabric as a pattern to cut a matching back from the remaining piece of Jubilee fabric. Sew doll front to back with right sides together, using a 1/2-inch seam and leaving an opening to turn.

Clip the corners and curves; turn right side out. Stuff the doll firmly with polyester fiberfill and sew the opening closed.

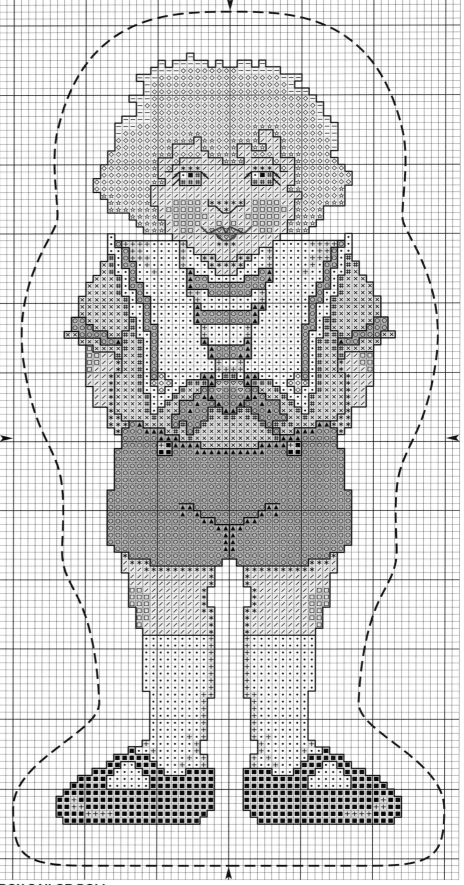

BOY SAILOR DOLL

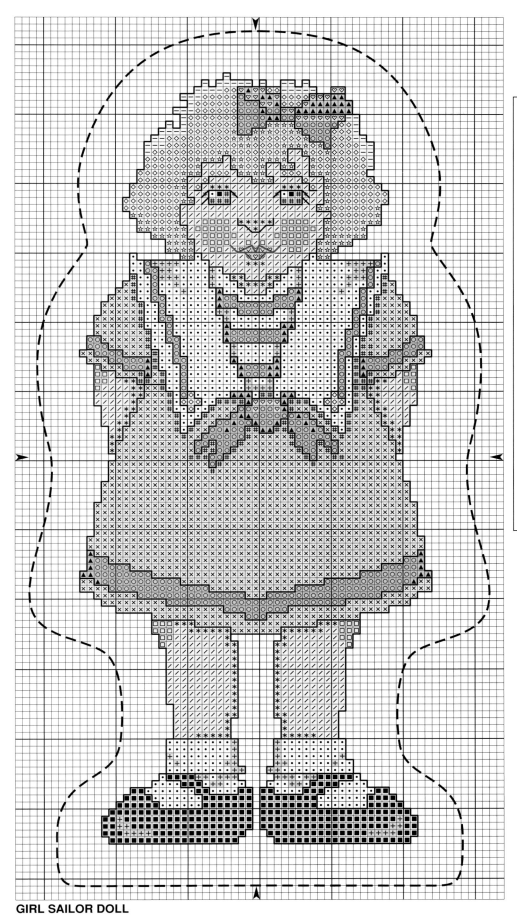

GIRL SAILOR DOLL

SAILOR DOLLS

ANCHOR		DMC	
002	·	000	White
403	■	310	Black
9046	⊙	321	Christmas red
374	+	415	Pearl gray
050	▢	605	Cranberry
305	☆	725	True topaz
295	◇	726	Light topaz
293	−	727	Pale topaz
1012	╱	754	Peach
882	✳	758	Terra cotta
136	⌗	799	Medium Delft blue
130	✕	809	True Delft blue
1005	▲	816	Garnet
076	♡	961	Rose pink

BACKSTITCH

403	╱	310 Black−all remaining stitches (1X)
9046	╱	321 Christmas red−mouths (1X)

Girl stitch count: 111 high x 49 wide
Girl finished design sizes:
14-count fabric – 8 x 3½ inches
11-count fabric – 10⅛ x 4½ inches
18-count fabric – 6¼ x 2¾ inches

Boy stitch count: 111 high x 48 wide
Boy finished design sizes:
14-count fabric – 8 x 3½ inches
11-count fabric –10⅛ x 4⅜ inches
18-count fabric – 6¼ x 2⅔ inches

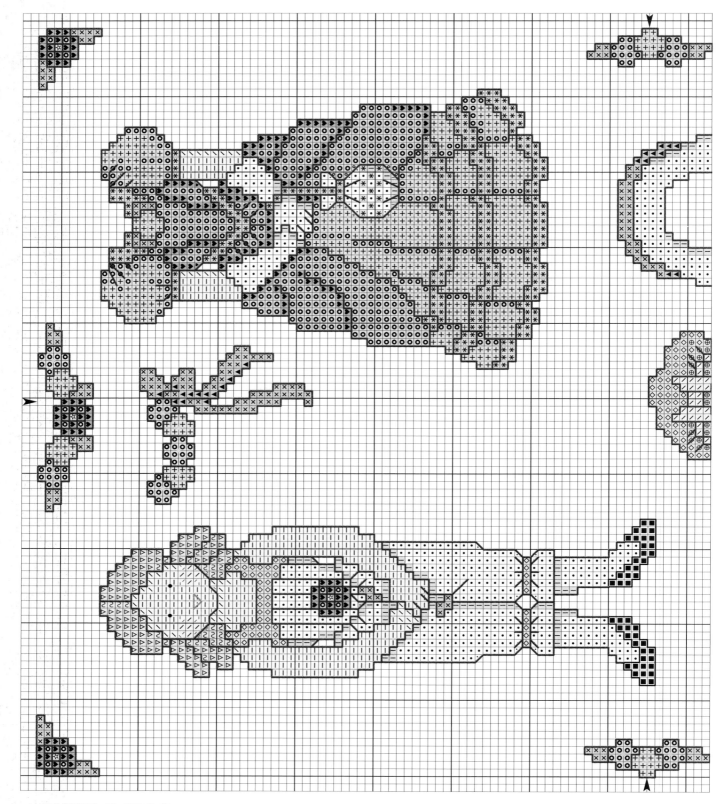

★ PAPER DOLLS

As shown on page 94.

MATERIALS *for framed piece or individual cutout pieces*

Fabric

9 x 12-inch piece of 14-count white perforated paper

Threads

Cotton embroidery floss in colors listed in key on page 101

#8 braid as listed in key on page 101

Supplies

Needle

Desired frame and mat

INSTRUCTIONS

For framed piece, find the center of the chart and the center of the perforated paper; begin stitching there. Use three plies of floss or one strand of braid to work all the cross-stitches. Work the French knots using

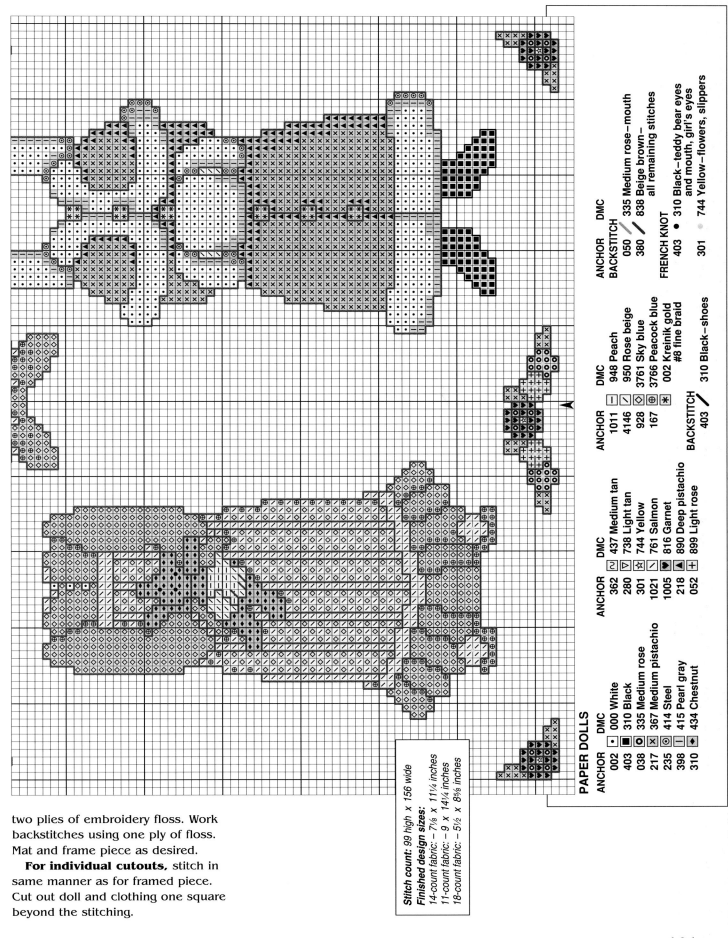

Stitch count: *99 high x 156 wide*
Finished design sizes:
14-count fabric: – 7⅛ x 11¼ inches
11-count fabric: – 9 x 14¼ inches
18-count fabric: – 5½ x 8⅝ inches

PAPER DOLLS

ANCHOR		DMC	
002	•	000	White
403	■	310	Black
038	◉	335	Medium rose
217	✕	367	Medium pistachio
235	◉	414	Steel
398	—	415	Pearl gray
310	◆	434	Chestnut

ANCHOR		DMC	
362	⊇	437	Medium tan
280	▷	738	Light tan
301	☆	744	Yellow
1021	╱	761	Salmon
1005	▶	816	Garnet
218	◀	890	Deep pistachio
052	╋	899	Light rose

ANCHOR		DMC	
1011	▯	948	Peach
4146	╱	950	Rose beige
928	⊕	3761	Sky blue
167	✳	3766	Peacock blue
		002	Kreinik gold #8 fine braid

BACKSTITCH
| 403 | ╱ | 310 | Black–shoes |

ANCHOR		DMC	
BACKSTITCH			
050	╱	335	Medium rose–mouth
380	╱	838	Beige brown– all remaining stitches
FRENCH KNOT			
403	●	310	Black–teddy bear eyes and mouth, girl's eyes
301	○	744	Yellow–flowers, slippers

two plies of embroidery floss. Work backstitches using one ply of floss. Mat and frame piece as desired.

For individual cutouts, stitch in same manner as for framed piece. Cut out doll and clothing one square beyond the stitching.

★★ CIRCUS PULL TOYS

As shown on page 95; lion is 4¼ inches tall, elephant is 3 inches tall, and giraffe is 4½ inches tall.

MATERIALS

For each pull toy

Fabric

Four 5 x 5-inch pieces of 14-count clear perforated plastic

2 x 4-inch piece of 14-count clear perforated plastic for base

Floss

Cotton embroidery floss in colors listed in key on page 103

Supplies

Needle

Four ⅝-inch-diameter buttons in desired color

Four ⅛-inch-diameter white buttons

Four ⅞-inch-diameter heart-shaped, star-shaped, or sun-shaped buttons

4¼-inch-long piece of #5 black pearl cotton

One ¼-inch-diameter wooden bead in desired color

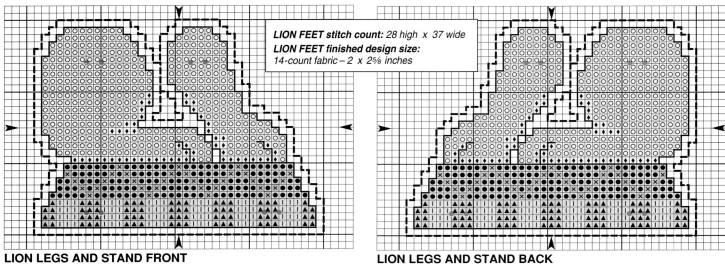

LION FEET stitch count: *28 high x 37 wide*
LION FEET finished design size:
14-count fabric – 2 x 2⅝ inches

LION LEGS AND STAND FRONT

LION LEGS AND STAND BACK

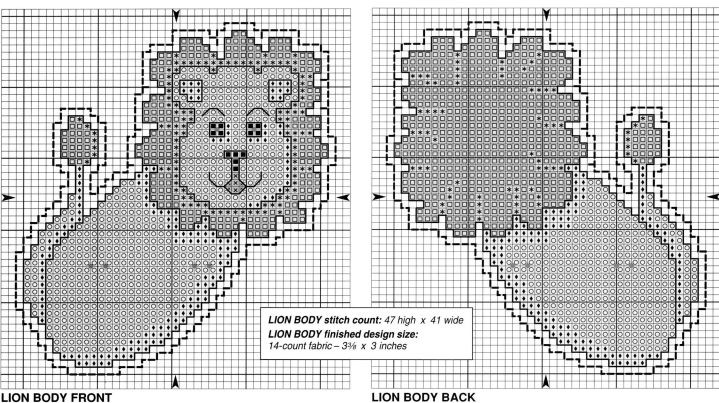

LION BODY stitch count: *47 high x 41 wide*
LION BODY finished design size:
14-count fabric – 3⅜ x 3 inches

LION BODY FRONT

LION BODY BACK

LION BASE

INSTRUCTIONS

Find the center of the desired chart and the center of one piece of plastic; begin stitching there. Use three plies of embroidery floss to work all the cross-stitches. Work the French knots as specified in key. Work backstitches using one ply of floss. Stitch the remaining charts in the same manner. Trim the perforated plastic one square beyond the stitched area of the design as indicated on the chart. Cut the base from small piece of plastic.

Whipstitch body front to the back using three plies of matching floss. Overcast the outside edges of the legs using three plies of embroidery

ELEPHANT BODY stitch count: 29 high x 50 wide
ELEPHANT BODY finished design size:
14-count fabric – 2 x 3½ inches
ELEPHANT FEET stitch count: 31 high x 31 wide
ELEPHANT FEET finished design size:
14-count fabric – 2⅛ x 2⅛ inches

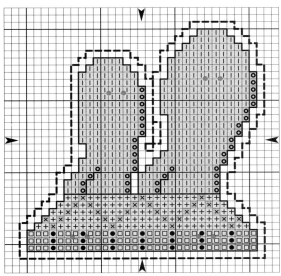

ELEPHANT LEGS AND STAND FRONT

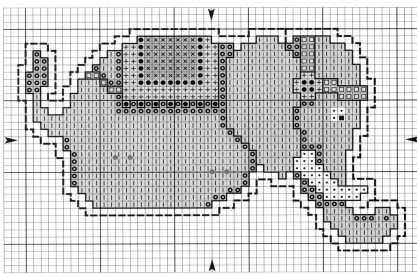

ELEPHANT BODY BACK

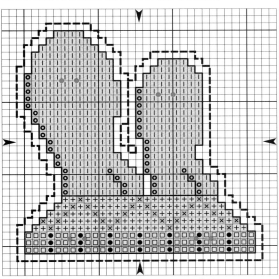

ELEPHANT LEGS AND STAND BACK

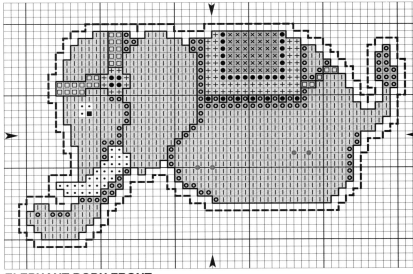

ELEPHANT BODY FRONT

CIRCUS PULL TOYS

ANCHOR		DMC	
002	⋅	000	White
289	○	307	True lemon
403	■	310	Black
9046	✕	321	Christmas red
290	◆	444	Medium lemon
088	◎	718	Plum
316	✳	740	Dark tangerine
314	☐	741	Medium tangerine
256	▲	906	Medium parrot green
255	✚	907	Light parrot green

ANCHOR		DMC	
410	●	995	Electric blue
087	I	3607	Fuchsia

BACKSTITCH
| 403 | ╱ | 310 Black – all stitches (1X) |

FRENCH KNOT
| 002 | • | 000 White – lion and giraffe eyes (1X) |

BUTTON PLACEMENT
| | • | |

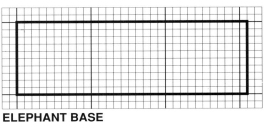

ELEPHANT BASE

GIRAFFE FEET stitch count: 32 high x 33 wide
GIRAFFE FEET finished design size:
14-count fabric – 2¼ x 2⅜ inches

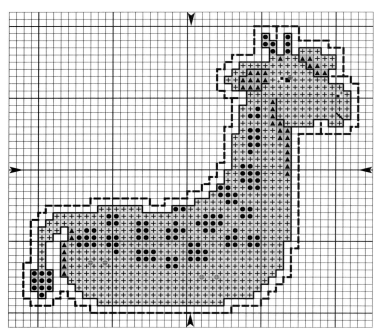

GIRAFFE BODY BACK

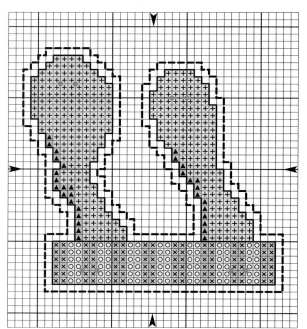

GIRAFFE LEGS AND STAND FRONT

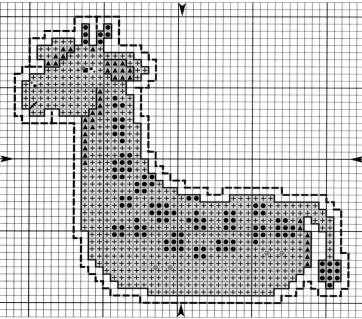

GIRAFFE BODY FRONT

GIRAFFE BODY stitch count: 38 high x 43 wide
GIRAFFE BODY finished design size:
14-count fabric – 2¾ x 3 inches

GIRAFFE LEGS AND STAND BACK

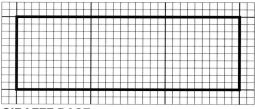

GIRAFFE BASE

floss. Whipstitch the base to the long straight edges of the leg pieces in the same manner. Position the body between the leg pieces. Join with small white buttons sewn at the marked spots.

For wheels, sew the button pairs to the bottom of the figure using three plies of embroidery floss.

For pull string, tie a 4-inch piece of black pearl cotton to the center front of the base. Tie a wooden bead to the end of the pearl cotton.

CANDYLAND CHECKERS GAME

As shown on pages 96–97.

★ ★ CHECKERS GAMEBOARD

MATERIALS
Fabric
20½ x 20½-inch piece of 14-count teal green Royal Classic fabric
Threads
Cotton embroidery floss and #8 braid in colors listed in key on page 106
Supplies
Needle; embroidery hoop
Green sewing thread

INSTRUCTIONS
Machine-stitch ¾ inch from all four edges of the fabric. Find the center of the chart, *pages 106–107,* and the center of the fabric; begin stitching there.

Use six plies of embroidery floss to work all the cross-stitches over two threads of fabric. Work the straight stitches using one ply and the French knots using two plies. Work the backstitches using three plies of floss. Remove the threads between the edges and the machine stitches for fringe. Press the finished stitchery from the back.

★ GAME PIECES

MATERIALS
For twenty-four game pieces
Fabrics
24 3 x 3-inch pieces of 14-count clear perforated plastic

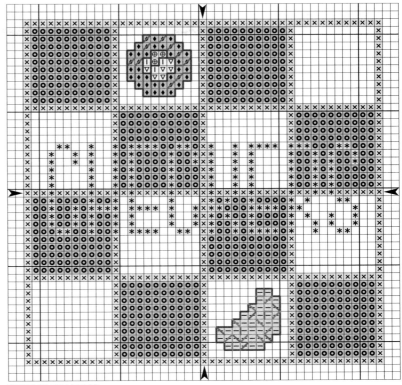

STORAGE BOX

Floss
Cotton embroidery floss in colors listed in key on page 106
Supplies
Needle

INSTRUCTIONS
Find the center of one piece of the perforated plastic and the center of the airplane or horse motif on the border of the checkers gameboard chart, *pages 106–107.* Use three plies of cotton embroidery floss to work all of the cross-stitches. Work the backstitches using two plies of embroidery floss.

Trim the perforated plastic one square beyond the stitched area of the design. Stitch twelve airplane and twelve horse game pieces.

★ ★ STORAGE BOX

MATERIALS
Fabric
10 x 10-inch piece of 14-count teal green Royal Classic fabric

Threads
Cotton embroidery floss in colors listed in the key on page 106
Gold braid as listed in the key on page 106
Supplies
Needle
Embroidery hoop
6¼ x 6¼-inch wooden box

INSTRUCTIONS
Tape or zigzag the edges of the 14-count teal green Royal Classic fabric to prevent them from fraying. Find the center of the chart, *above,* and the center of the fabric; begin stitching design there.

Use three plies of the cotton embroidery floss or one strand of the gold braid to work all of the cross-stitches over one thread of fabric. Work the straight stitches and the backstitches using one ply of floss. Assemble the box following the manufacturer's instructions provided with the box.

CANDYLAND CHECKERS GAME

ANCHOR		DMC	
002	⊡	000	White
109	◇	209	Lavender
9046	◉	321	Christmas red
398	☒	415	Pearl gray
1046	⊙	435	Chestnut
362	⊟	437	Tan
288	⊞	445	Lemon
099	●	552	Violet
228	◆	700	Medium Christmas green
226	⌗	702	Light Christmas green
238	○	703	Chartreuse
295	▽	726	Topaz
303	⊕	742	Tangerine
043	▲	815	Garnet
360	◆	839	Beige brown
382	■	3371	Black brown
035	✛	3801	Watermelon
	✳	002	Kreinik gold #8 fine braid

BACKSTITCH

002	╱	000	White—lines on gingerbread men
9046	╱	321	Christmas red— gingerbread men's smile
050	╱	605	Cranberry—icing lines on box lid
382	╱	3371	Black brown—all remaining stitches lid (1X); mat (3X)

STRAIGHT STITCH

9046	╱	321	Christmas red— sprinkles on almond crescent on box lid
226	╱	702	Light Christmas green— sprinkles on almond crescent on box lid

FRENCH KNOT

002	●	000	White—sugar sprinkles on fruit slices
9046	●	321	Christmas red— gingerbread men corners of smile

MAT stitch count: 129 high x 129 wide
MAT finished design sizes:
14-count fabric – 9¼ x 9¼ inches
LID stitch count: 45 high x 45 wide
LID finished design sizes:
14-count fabric – 3¼ x 3¼ inches
GAME PIECES stitch count: 15 high x 15 wide
GAME PIECES finished design sizes:
14-count fabric – 1 x 1 inch

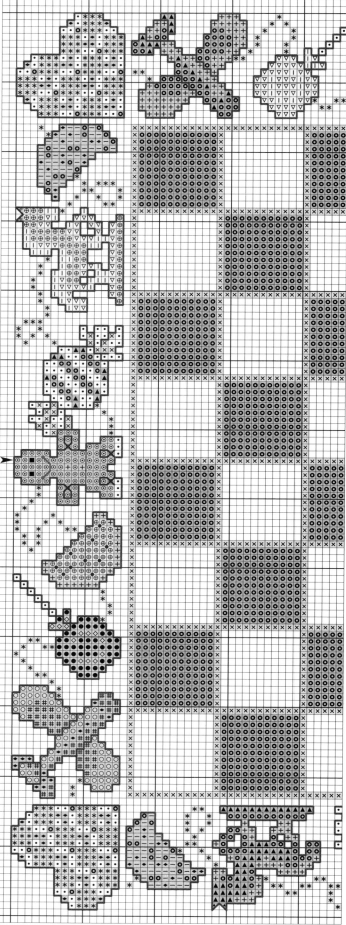

CHECKERS GAMEBOARD

TREASURED KEEPSAKES

Each Christmas we eagerly unpack and display our favorite holiday accessories. Create these elegant cross-stitched pieces to add to your collection of treasured keepsakes.

This simple snowflake motif is repeated on 25-count Victorian green Lugana fabric to create our classic *Snowflake Ribbon.* The snowflakes are stitched with silver metallic thread for extra sparkle. The complete instructions and chart are on page 115.

Designer: Barbara Sestok ◆ Photographer: Scott Little

Victorian Ornaments

These dazzling ornaments are stitched on 28-count linen and use colorful rayon embroidery floss and metallic threads to add a special sparkle. They are finished with richly-colored cording and tassels to create beautiful Victorian-styled trims. The complete instructions and charts begin on page 115.

Designer: Barbara Sestok
Photographer: Hopkins Associates

Hardanger Ornaments

These Hardanger ornaments are delicately stitched using white pearl cotton or overdyed floss and will make charming additions to any tree. The red snowflake ornament has a pretty silver button in the center of the design and the white ornament has a Christmas tree motif that has been repeated to form a geometric design. The complete instructions and charts begin on page 117.

Designer: Carole Rodgers ◆ Photographer: Scott Little

Hardanger Tree

Stitch this Hardanger Christmas tree sampler on 32-count ivory linen just in time
for the holiday season. Simple stitches work up quickly to create this elegant piece.
For variation, try choosing two different colors to work the design. The complete
instructions and chart begin on page 119.

Designer: Patricia Andrle ◆ Photographer: Scott Little

Poinsettia Wreath

The poinsettia is a traditional flower symbolizing Christmastime. This pretty wreath, featuring this elegant bloom, will provide a warm welcome to guests during the holiday season. The motifs are worked entirely with whole stitches on 28-count white linen. Complete instructions and chart are on pages 120–121.

Designer: Jim Williams ◆ Photographer: Scott Little

Holly Tree Mini-Sampler

This seasonal mini-sampler stitches up easily on 14-count white Aida cloth. The holly motif is repeated around an alphabet and a Christmas tree. Propped on a mantel surrounded by greenery or hanging on the wall—the piece will add a festive touch to your home. Complete instructions and chart begin on page 122.

Designer: Ursula Michael ◆ Photographer: Hopkins Associates

Holly Table Runner

Bring Christmas cheer to your table when you adorn it with this beautiful table runner. A bright red bow is the center of attention with sprigs of holly and evergreen stitched on 20-count silver-and-white Valerie fabric. Finish the piece with a delicate white lace trim. Complete instructions and chart begin on page 122.

Designer: Jim Williams ◆ Photographer: Scott Little

★SNOWFLAKE RIBBON

As shown on page 108, finished ribbon is 2⅛ inches wide.

MATERIALS
Fabrics
5-inch-wide piece of 25-count Victorian green Lugana fabric in desired length

1¾-inch-wide piece of white lightweight fusible interfacing in desired length

Thread
Metallic silver embroidery thread

Supplies
Needle; embroidery hoop

INSTRUCTIONS
Tape or zigzag the edges of the 25-count Victorian green Lugana fabric to prevent them from fraying. Find the vertical center of the chart and the vertical center of the fabric. Measure 1 inch from one end of the Lugana strip; begin stitching design there over two threads. Use one strand of the silver metallic embroidery thread to work the French knots, straight stitches, and backstitches. Continue stitching the snowflake pattern until the desired length is reached. Centering design, trim fabric to measure 3⅛ inches wide. Trim the short ends 1 inch from the stitching.

Press the edges under ½ inch on all sides of the Lugana strip. Center the white lightweight fusible interfacing onto the back of the stitchery with the interfacing over the pressed edges of the Lugana strip. Fuse following manufacturer's instructions.

VICTORIAN ORNAMENTS

As shown on page 111. Diamond ornament measures 5x5 inches; heart ornament measures 4½ x 4½ inches.

★★★ DIAMOND-SHAPED VICTORIAN ORNAMENT
MATERIALS
Fabrics
6x6-inch piece of 28-count autumn leaf linen

5x5-inch piece of white felt

SNOWFLAKE RIBBON

ANCHOR	DMC	
BACKSTITCH		
╱	283	Silver metallic – all backstitches
STRAIGHT STITCH		
╱	283	Silver metallic – all straight stitches
FRENCH KNOT		
●	283	Silver metallic – all French knots

Stitch count: 36 high x 22 wide

Finished design sizes:
25-count fabric – 2⅞ x 1¾ inches
11-count fabric – 3⅜ x 2 inches
18-count fabric – 2 x 1¼ inches

Threads
Rayon embroidery floss in colors listed in key on page 116

DMC metallic gold embroidery thread

Supplies
Needle

Embroidery hoop

Gold seed beads; tracing paper

Erasable fabric marker; crafts glue

5x5-inch piece of self-stick mounting board with foam

12-inch piece *each* of ¼-inch-wide gold cord, white rattail cord, and ¾-inch-wide picot-edged gold trim

5-inch piece of ⅛-inch-diameter metallic gold cord

Purchased 3-inch-long gold tassel

Two purchased 2-inch-long gold tassels

INSTRUCTIONS
Tape or zigzag edges of linen to prevent fraying. Find center of chart and of fabric; begin stitching there. Use two plies of floss to work cross-stitches over two threads. Work backstitches using one strand of metallic thread. Attach beads using one ply.

Use erasable marker to draw ornament outline on fabric as indicated by dotted line on chart; *do not* cut out. Place tracing paper over fabric; trace ornament outline. Use tracing paper pattern to cut one shape each from mounting board and felt.

Peel protective paper from the mounting board. Center the foam side on the back of the stitchery and press to stick. Trim the excess fabric ½ inch beyond edges of board. Fold raw edges of fabric to back and glue.

Glue rattail cord around front of ornament. Glue gold cord behind rattail. Glue gold trim behind gold cord. Fold narrow gold cord in half and glue ends of the cord to one point of ornament. Glue large tassel to opposite point of ornament. Glue small tassels to side points of ornament. Glue felt to back of ornament.

★★★ HEART-SHAPED VICTORIAN ORNAMENT
MATERIALS
Fabrics
6x6-inch piece of 28-count ruby linen

4x4-inch piece of burgundy felt

Threads
Rayon embroidery floss in colors listed in key on page 116

DMC metallic gold embroidery thread

Supplies
Needle; embroidery hoop

Gold seed beads; tracing paper

Erasable fabric marker; crafts glue

5x5-inch piece of self-stick glue mounting board with foam

14-inch piece of ¼-inch-diameter burgundy-and-gold twisted cord

Two 5-inch pieces of ⅛-inch-diameter metallic gold cord

INSTRUCTIONS

Tape or zigzag the edges of the fabric to prevent fraying. Find the center of the chart and the center of the fabric; begin stitching there. Use two plies of floss to work the cross-stitches over two threads of fabric. Work the backstitches using one strand of metallic thread. Attach the gold seed beads using one ply of matching embroidery floss.

Use the erasable fabric marker to draw the ornament outline on the fabric as indicated by the dotted line on the chart; *do not* cut out. Place the tracing paper over the fabric and trace the ornament outline. Use the tracing paper pattern to cut one shape from the self-stick mounting board and one shape from the burgundy felt.

Peel the protective paper from the mounting board. Center the foam side on the back of the stitchery and press to stick. Trim the excess fabric ½ inch beyond the edges of the board. Fold the raw edges of the fabric to the back and glue.

Glue gold trim around edge of the heart. Glue the burgundy-and-gold cord behind the gold trim. Tie one piece of the narrow gold cord into a bow; glue to the top center of the heart. Fold the remaining piece of the gold cord in half; glue the ends of the cord to the top center of the ornament. Glue the felt to the back of the ornament.

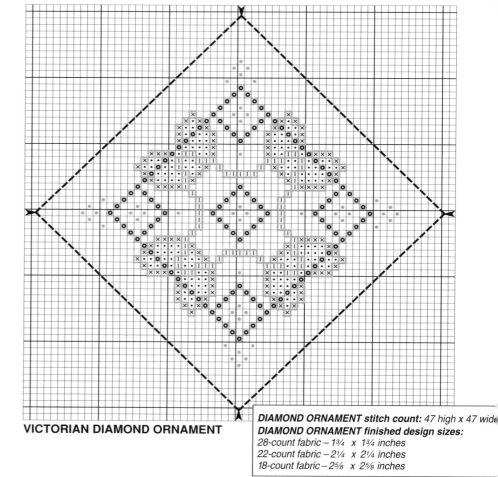

VICTORIAN DIAMOND ORNAMENT

DIAMOND ORNAMENT stitch count: 47 high x 47 wide
DIAMOND ORNAMENT finished design sizes:
28-count fabric – 1¾ x 1¾ inches
22-count fabric – 2¼ x 2¼ inches
18-count fabric – 2⅝ x 2⅝ inches

VICTORIAN ORNAMENTS

MARLITT	ANCHOR		DMC	
800	(002)	·	(000)	White
1207	(895)	+	(223)	Shell pink
894	(1005)	▲	(498)	Christmas red
848	(302)	✕	(743)	True yellow
1013	(300)	I	(745)	Light yellow
1079	(309)	◉	(781)	Topaz

BACKSTITCH

                 282 Gold metallic thread – all stitches

BEADS

     361   •   738 Tan (2X) and 5142 Wichelt Dark gold whimsy bead – all beads

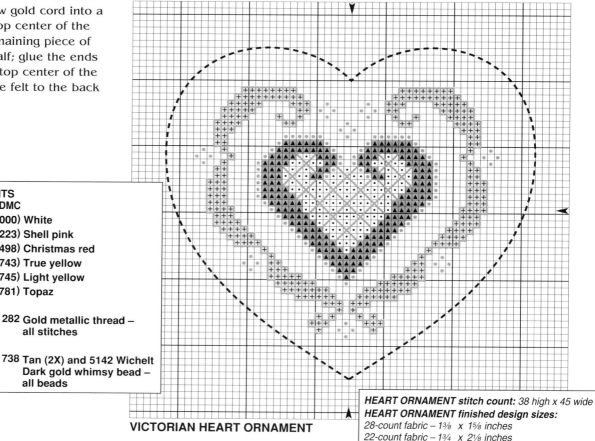

VICTORIAN HEART ORNAMENT

HEART ORNAMENT stitch count: 38 high x 45 wide
HEART ORNAMENT finished design sizes:
28-count fabric – 1⅜ x 1⅝ inches
22-count fabric – 1¾ x 2⅛ inches
18-count fabric – 2⅛ x 2½ inches

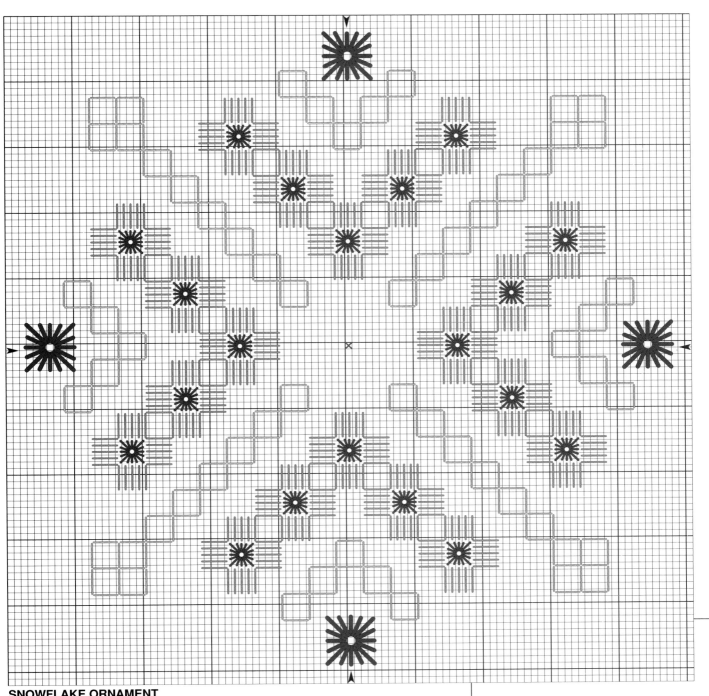

SNOWFLAKE ORNAMENT

HARDANGER ORNAMENTS

As shown on page 110, ornaments are 3-3/4 x 3-3/4 inches.

★★ HARDANGER
SNOWFLAKE ORNAMENT

MATERIALS

Fabrics

Two 6x6-inch pieces of 25-count Victorian red Lugana fabric

Threads

#5 white pearl cotton
#8 silver braid

Supplies

Size 24 tapestry needle

Embroidery hoop

3-1/4 x 3-1/4-inch piece of self-stick mounting board with foam

Ruler; pencil; awl

3 x 3-inch piece of self-stick mounting board

9-inch piece of Kreinik 1/8-inch-wide metallic silver ribbon

Scissors; crafts glue

3/4-inch-diameter poinsettia-designed silver button

SATIN STITCH

╱   White pearl cotton #5

ALGERIAN EYELETS

✳   001 Silver Kreinik #8 fine braid

FOUR-SIDED BACKSTITCH

☐   001 Silver Kreinik #8 fine braid

BUTTON PLACEMENT

✕   Silver button

Stitch count: 98 high x 97 wide
Finished design sizes:
25-count fabric – 4 x 3⅞ inches
22-count fabric – 4½ x 4⅜ inches

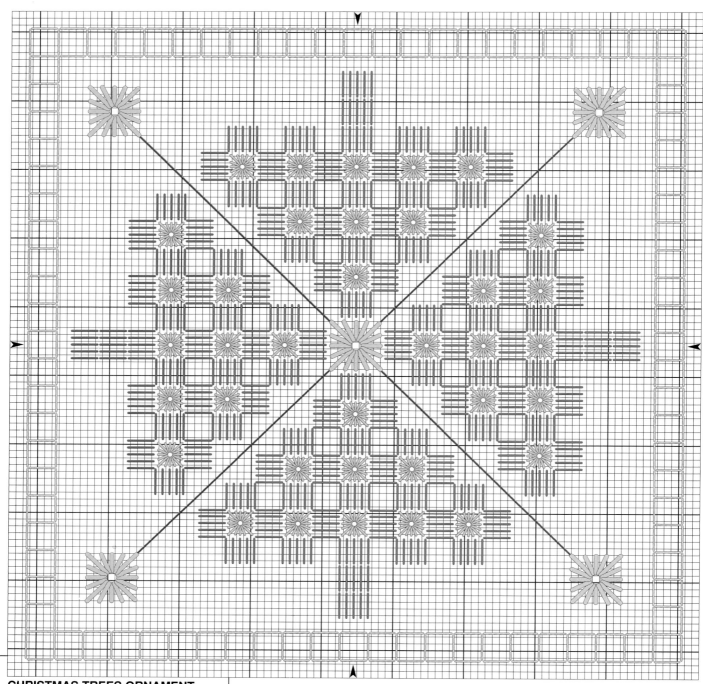

CHRISTMAS TREES ORNAMENT

SATIN STITCH

/ 083 Pine forest

BACKSTITCH

/ 002 Gold Kreinik #8 fine braid

ALGERIAN EYELETS

※ 002 Gold Kreinik #8 fine braid

FOUR-SIDED BACKSTITCH

▢ 002 Gold Kreinik #8 fine braid

Stitch count: 93 high x 92 wide
Finished design sizes:
25-count fabric – 3¾ x 3⅝ inches
22-count fabric – 4¼ x 4⅛ inches

INSTRUCTIONS

Tape or zigzag edges of one piece of Victorian red Lugana fabric to prevent fraying. Find center of chart and center of the fabric; begin stitching there. Work all stitches over number of threads indicated on chart using one strand of thread. Press finished stitchery from back and set aside.

Find the center of the self-stick foam mounting board by measuring diagonally corner to corner; mark a small x. Use the awl to punch a small hole on each side of the x.

Peel the protective paper from the mounting board. Center the foam side on the back of the stitched design and press to stick. Peel the protective paper from the remaining mounting board, center on remaining piece of fabric, and press to stick. Trim each piece of fabric to within ½ inch from edge of cardboard. Fold the raw edges to the back. Glue with the crafts glue, mitering the corners as needed.

Sew the button to the center front of design through the holes in the cardboard; pull the thread tightly, pulling the shank into one hole to indent the fabric.

For the hanger, fold the 9-inch piece of 1/8-inch-wide metallic silver ribbon in half and glue the ends to the back of the stitched design at one corner. Glue the fabric-covered boards together.

★★ HARDANGER CHRISTMAS TREES ORNAMENT
MATERIALS
Fabric
Two 6 x 6-inch pieces of 25-count white Lugana fabric
Thread
Caron Watercolors floss in color listed in key on page 118
Braid as listed in key on page 118
Supplies
Size 24 tapestry needle
Embroidery hoop
3¼ x 3¼-inch piece of self-stick mounting board with foam
3 x 3-inch piece of self-stick mounting board
9-inch piece of Kreinik #32 gold braid
Crafts glue

INSTRUCTIONS
Tape or zigzag the edges of one piece of the fabric to prevent fraying. Find the center of the chart and the center of the fabric; begin stitching there. Work all of the stitches over the number of threads indicated on the chart using one strand of floss or one strand of braid. Press the stitchery and set aside.

Peel the protective paper from the mounting board. Center the foam side on the back of the stitched design and press to stick. Peel the protective paper from the remaining mounting board, center it on the remaining piece of the fabric, and press to stick. Trim each piece of the fabric to within ½ inch from the edge of the cardboard. Fold the raw edges to the back. Glue with the crafts glue, mitering the corners as needed.

For the hanger, fold the 9-inch piece of #32 gold braid in half and glue the ends to the back of the stitched design at one corner. Glue the fabric-covered boards together.

★★★★ HARDANGER TREE
As shown on page 111.
MATERIALS
Fabric
11 x 11-inch-wide piece of 32-count ivory linen
Floss
Cotton embroidery floss in colors listed in key
Supplies
Needle
Embroidery hoop
Desired frame and mat

INSTRUCTIONS
Tape or zigzag edges of fabric to prevent fraying. Find the center of the chart and the center of the fabric; begin stitching there. Refer to diagrams, *right,* to work all specialty stitches using three plies of floss.

Center and stitch desired initials and date using the small chart *below,* referring to the sampler chart for placement. Press the finished stitchery from the back. Mat and frame the piece as desired.

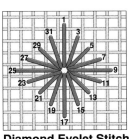
Diamond Eyelet Stitch

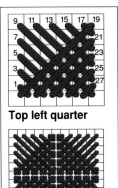
Top left quarter

Satin Cushion Stitch

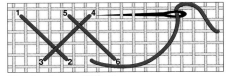
Herringbone Stitch

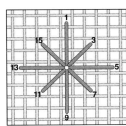
Star Stitch

Satin Stitch

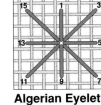
Algerian Eyelet

Double Cross Stitch

Rice Stitch

HARDANGER TREE SAMPLER ALPHABET

HARDANGER TREE SAMPLER		
ANCHOR	**DMC**	
002 ·	000 White	
212 ▲	561 Dark seafoam	
210 ◯	562 Medium seafoam	
BACKSTITCH		
212 /	561 Dark seafoam— all backstitches (1X)	
ALGERIAN EYELETS		
002 ✳	000 White – inside tree border and row 3 (3X)	
DIAMOND EYELETS		
002 ✳	000 White – row 1 (3X)	
HERRINGBONE STITCH		
002 ✕✕	000 White – row 2 and row 8 (3X)	

ANCHOR	DMC
SATIN STITCHES	
002 /	000 White – row 3, row 5 and row 9 (3X)
SATIN CUSHION STITCH	
002 ▨	000 White – row 9 (3X)
DOUBLE CROSS STITCH	
002 ✳	000 White – row 4 (3X)
RICE STITCH	
002 ✕✕	000 White – row 6 (3X)
DOUBLE RICE STITCH	
002 ✕✕	000 White – row 7 (3X)
STAR STITCH	
002 ✳	000 White – row 9 (3X)

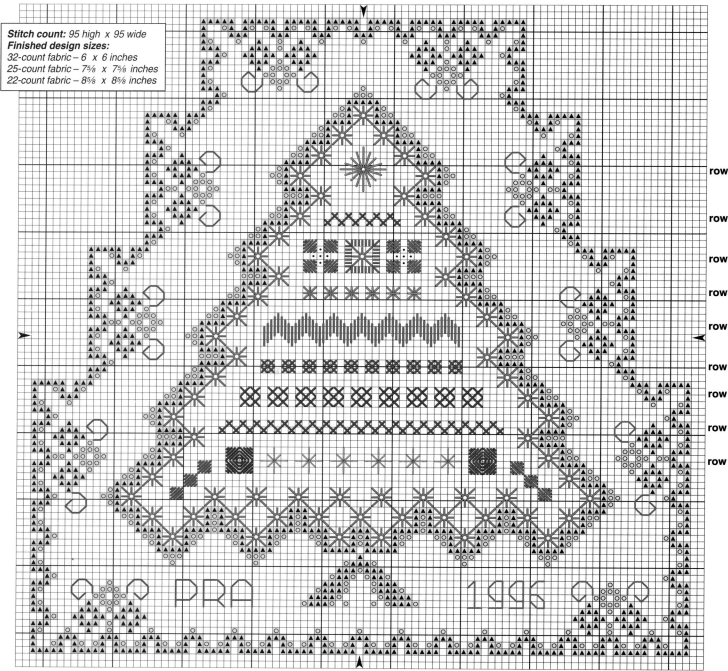

Stitch count: 95 high x 95 wide
Finished design sizes:
32-count fabric – 6 x 6 inches
25-count fabric – 7⅝ x 7⅝ inches
22-count fabric – 8⅝ x 8⅝ inches

row
row
row
row
row
row
row
row
row

HARDANGER TREE SAMPLER

★★★ POINSETTIA WREATH

As shown on page 112.

MATERIALS

Fabric

20 x 20-inch piece of 28-count white linen

Floss

Cotton embroidery floss in colors listed in key on page 121

Supplies

Needle; embroidery hoop

Basting thread
Desired frame and mat

INSTRUCTIONS

Tape or zigzag the edges of the linen to prevent fraying. Use the basting thread to divide the linen into quarters. Find the center marking on the chart and the center of the fabric; begin stitching there. Use three plies of floss to work all cross-stitches over two threads of fabric.

Stitch the entire chart to complete one quarter of the design. When the first quarter is complete, rotate the fabric a quarter turn (90°) and stitch the second quarter aligning the points that are indicated by the black outlined areas on the chart on page 121. Stitch the remaining design, rotating 90° after each quarter is stitched. Press the finished stitchery from the back. Mat and frame the piece as desired.

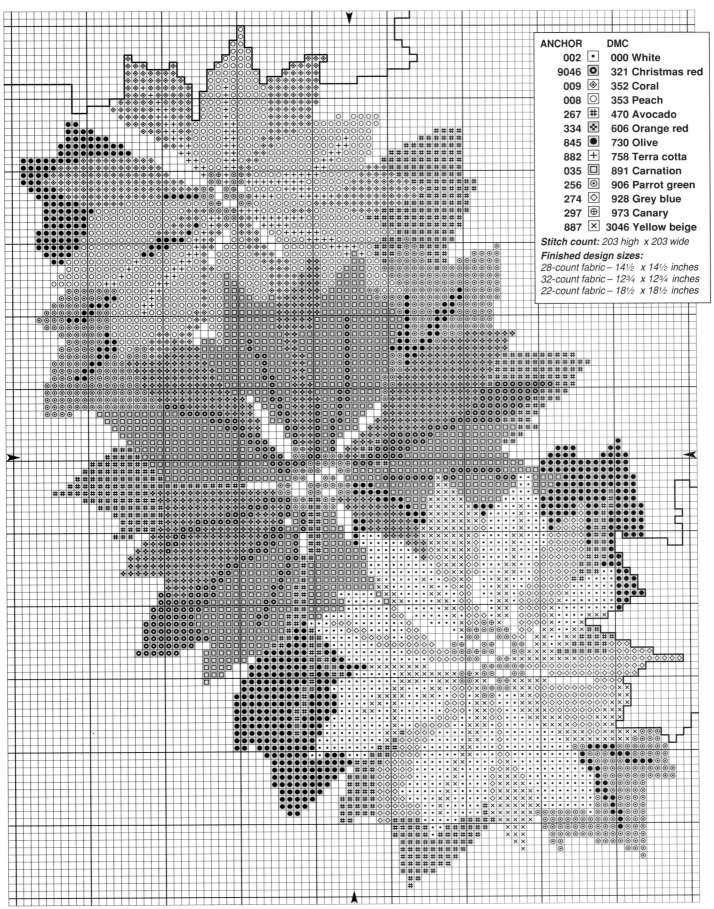

ANCHOR		DMC	
002	·	000	White
9046	◉	321	Christmas red
009	◈	352	Coral
008	○	353	Peach
267	⊞	470	Avocado
334	❖	606	Orange red
845	●	730	Olive
882	+	758	Terra cotta
035	▢	891	Carnation
256	⊙	906	Parrot green
274	◇	928	Grey blue
297	⊕	973	Canary
887	✕	3046	Yellow beige

Stitch count: 203 high x 203 wide
Finished design sizes:
28-count fabric – 14½ x 14½ inches
32-count fabric – 12¾ x 12¾ inches
22-count fabric – 18½ x 18½ inches

POINSETTIA WREATH

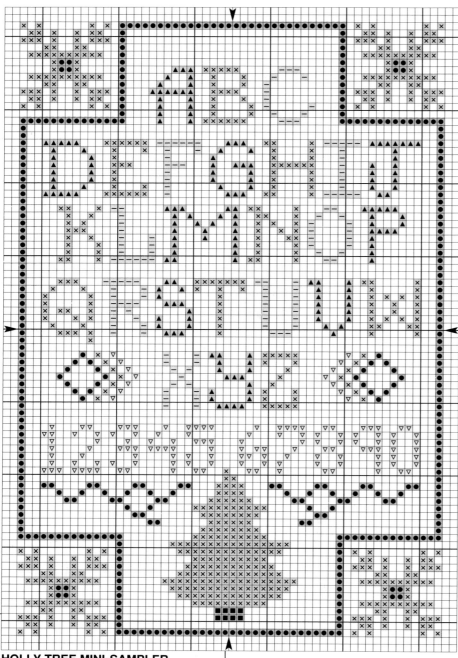

HOLLY TREE MINI-SAMPLER

ANCHOR		DMC	
9046	●	321	Christmas red
228	▲	700	Medium Christmas green
227	✕	701	True Christmas green
238	—	703	Chartreuse
305	▽	725	Topaz
1050	■	3781	Mocha

Stitch count: 84 high x 56 wide
Finished design sizes:
14-count fabric – 6 x 4 inches
11-count fabric – 7⅝ x 5⅛ inches
18-count fabric – 4⅝ x 3⅛ inches

★ HOLLY TREE MINI-SAMPLER

As shown on page 113.

MATERIALS

Fabric
14 x 14-inch piece of 14-count
   white Aida cloth

Floss
Cotton embroidery floss in colors
   listed in key

Supplies
Needle
Embroidery hoop
Desired frame and mat

INSTRUCTIONS

Tape or zigzag the edges of the
fabric to prevent fraying. Find the
center of the chart and the center of
the fabric; begin stitching there. Use
three plies of floss to work the cross-
stitches. Press the finished stitchery
from the back. Mat and frame the
piece as desired.

★★ HOLLY TABLE RUNNER

*As shown on page 114, table runner
measures 19 x 58 inches.*

MATERIALS

Fabrics
20 x 56-inch piece of 20-count
   silver-and-white Valerie fabric
16½ x 54-inch piece of polyester
   fleece
16½ x 54-inch piece of cotton lining
   fabric

Floss
Cotton embroidery floss in colors
   listed in key on page 123

Supplies
Needle; embroidery hoop
White sewing thread
3¾ yards of ⅛-inch-wide metallic
   silver piping
3¾ yards of 2-inch-wide flat white
   picot-edged lace

INSTRUCTIONS

Tape or zigzag edges of fabric to
prevent fraying. Find vertical center
of the chart and the vertical center of
fabric. Measure 1⅞ inches from one
end of fabric; begin stitching bottom
of holly stems there. Use three plies
of floss to work cross-stitches over
two threads of fabric. Work the backstitches using two plies. Repeat at
opposite end, extending red ribbon
to meet at center of fabric.

Trim fabric to 16½ x 54½ inches,
centering design and rounding the
corners. Baste the fleece to back of
Valerie using ¼-inch seams. Sew the

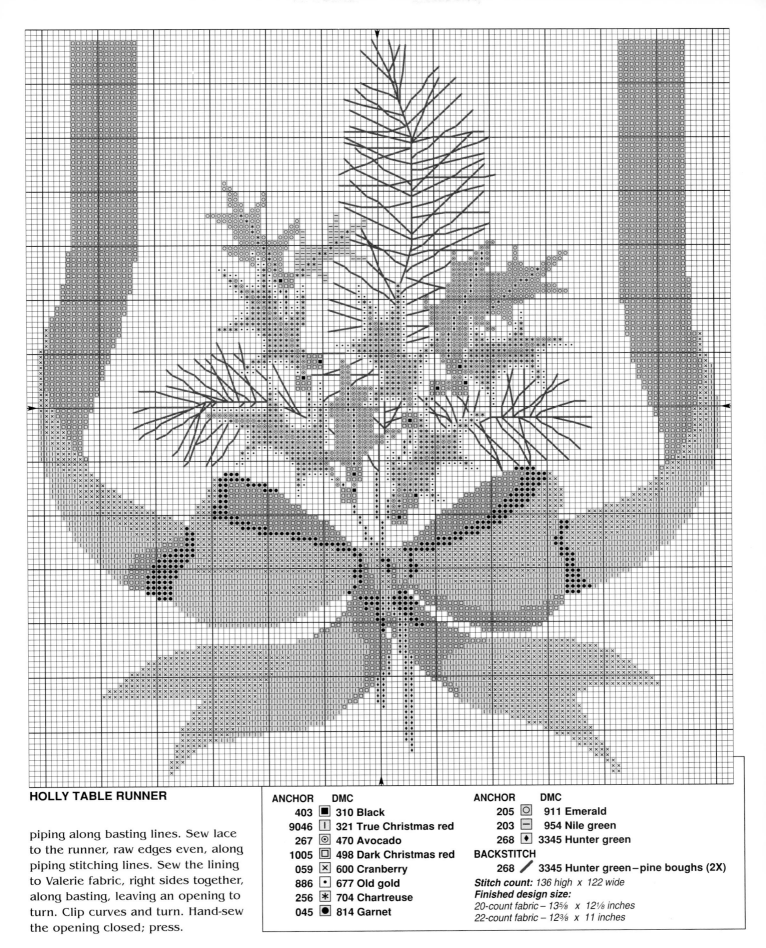

HOLLY TABLE RUNNER

piping along basting lines. Sew lace to the runner, raw edges even, along piping stitching lines. Sew the lining to Valerie fabric, right sides together, along basting, leaving an opening to turn. Clip curves and turn. Hand-sew the opening closed; press.

ANCHOR		DMC
403	■	310 Black
9046	Ι	321 True Christmas red
267	⊙	470 Avocado
1005	◻	498 Dark Christmas red
059	✕	600 Cranberry
886	•	677 Old gold
256	✳	704 Chartreuse
045	●	814 Garnet

ANCHOR		DMC
205	◯	911 Emerald
203	–	954 Nile green
268	◆	3345 Hunter green

BACKSTITCH

268	╱	3345 Hunter green – pine boughs (2X)

Stitch count: 136 high x 122 wide
Finished design size:
20-count fabric – 13⅝ x 12⅛ inches
22-count fabric – 12⅜ x 11 inches

CROSS-STITCH BASICS

Getting started

Cut the floss into 15- to 18-inch lengths and separate all six plies. Recombine the plies as indicated in the project instructions and thread into a blunt-tipped needle. Rely on project instructions to find out where to begin stitching the piece.

Basic cross-stitch

Make one cross-stitch for each symbol on the chart. For horizontal rows, stitch the first diagonal of each stitch in the row. Then, work back across the row, completing each stitch. On most linen and evenweave fabrics, stitches are worked over two threads as shown in the diagram, below. For Aida cloth, each stitch fills one square.

Cross-stitches also can be worked in the reverse direction. Just remember to embroider the stitches uniformly; that is, always work the top half of the stitch in the same direction.

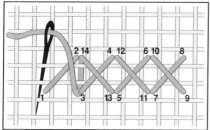

Basic Cross-Stitch in Rows

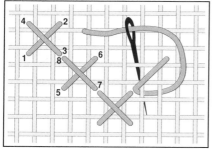

Basic Cross-Stitch Worked Individually

How to secure thread at beginning

The most common way to secure the beginning tail of thread is to hold it under the first four or five stitches.

Or, you can use a waste knot. Thread needle and knot end of thread. Insert needle from right side of fabric, about 4 inches away from placement of first stitch. Bring needle up through fabric and work first series of stitches. When stitching is finished, turn piece to right side and clip the knot. Rethread needle with excess floss and push needle through to the wrong side of stitchery.

When you work with two, four, or six plies of floss, use a loop knot. Cut half as many plies of thread, but make each one twice as long. Recombine plies, fold the strand in half, and thread all the ends into the needle. Work the first diagonal of the first stitch, then slip the needle through the loop formed by folding the thread.

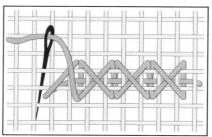

How to Secure Thread at Beginning

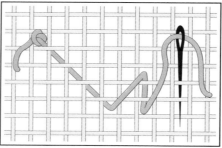

Waste Knot

How to secure thread at end

To finish, slip threaded needle under previously stitched threads on wrong side of fabric for four or five stitches, weaving thread back and forth a few times. Clip thread.

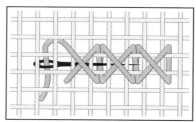

How to Secure Thread at End

Half stitches

A half cross-stitch is simply a single diagonal or half of a cross-stitch. Half cross-stitches are usually listed under a separate heading in the color key and are indicated on the chart by a diagonal colored line in the desired direction.

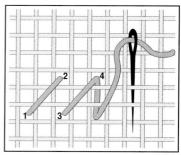

Half Cross-Stitch

Quarter and three-quarter stitches

Quarter and three-quarter stitches are used to obtain rounded shapes in a design. On linen and evenweave fabrics, a quarter stitch extends from the corner to the center intersection of threads. To make quarter stitches on Aida cloth, you'll have to estimate the center of the square. Three-quarter stitches combine a quarter stitch with a half cross-stitch. Both stitches may slant in any direction.

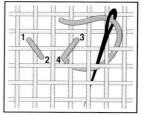

Quarter Cross-Stitch

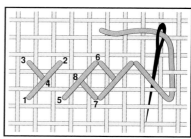

Three-Quarter Stitch

Cross-Stitches with beads

When beads are attached using a cross-stitch, work half cross-stitches and attach beads on the return stitch.

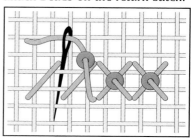

Cross-Stitch with Bead

Backstitches

Backstitches are added to define and outline the shapes in a design. For most projects, backstitches require only one ply of floss. On color key, (2X) indicates two plies of floss, (3X) indicates three plies, etc.

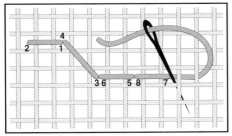

Backstitch

French knot

Bring threaded needle through fabric and wrap floss around the needle as illustrated. Tighten the twists and insert needle back through same place in the fabric. The floss will slide through the wrapped thread to make the knot.

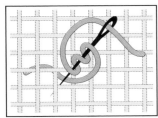

French Knot

Whipstitch

A whipstitch is an overcast stitch which is often used to finish edges on projects that use perforated plastic. The stitches are pulled tightly for a neatly finished edge. Whipstitches can also be used to join two fabrics together.

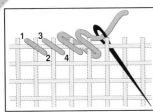

Whipstitch

CHART RATING

The rating system tells the degree of difficulty for each design. Find the star next to the project title.

Easy	★
Experienced	★★
Skilled	★★★
Expert	★★★★

MATERIALS FOR CROSS-STITCH

Counted cross-stitch has become a popular form of stitchery. Many stitchers like to work cross-stitch designs on different fabrics and use different threads than specified in the projects. Here is some information to help you understand the projects in this book and adapt them to your own needs.

Cross-stitch fabrics

Counted cross-stitch can be worked on any fabric that will enable you to make consistently sized, even stitches.

Aida cloth is the most popular of all cross-stitch fabrics. Threads are woven in groups separated by tiny spaces. This creates a pattern of squares across surface of fabric and enables a beginning stitcher to easily identify exactly where cross-stitches should be placed. Aida is measured by squares per inch; 14-count Aida has 14 squares per inch.

Aida cloth comes in many varieties. 100% cotton Aida cloth is available in thread counts 6, 8, 11, 14, 16, and 18. 14-count cotton Aida cloth is available in over 60 colors. For beginners, white Aida is available with a removable grid of pre-basted threads.

Linen is considered to be a standard of excellence fabric for experienced stitchers. The threads used to weave linen vary in thickness, giving linen fabrics a slightly irregular surface. When you purchase linen remember that the thread count is measured by threads per inch, but most designs are worked over two threads, so 28-count linen will yield 14 stitches per inch. Linens are made in counts from 14 (seven stitches per inch) to 40.

Evenweave fabric is also worked over two threads. Popularity of cross-stitch has created a market for specialty fabrics for counted cross-stitch. They are referred to as evenweave fabrics because they are woven from threads with a consistent diameter, even though some of these fabrics are woven to create a homespun look. Most evenweave fabrics are counted like linen, by threads per inch, and generally worked over two threads.

Hardanger fabric can be used for very fine counted cross-stitch. The traditional fabric for the Norwegian embroidery of the same name has an over-two, under-two weave that produces 22 small squares per inch.

Needlepoint canvas is frequently used for cross-stitching, especially on clothing and other fabrics that are not suitable alone. Waste canvas is designed to unravel when dampened. It ranges in count from 6½ to 20 stitches per inch. Cross-stitches can also be worked directly on mono needlepoint canvas. It is available in colors, and when background is left unstitched, it can create an interesting effect.

Sweaters and other knits are often worked in duplicate stitch from cross-stitch charts. Knit stitches are not square, they are wider than they are tall. A duplicate-stitched design will appear broader and shorter than the chart it was worked from.

Gingham or other simple plaid fabrics can be used, but gingham "squares" are not perfectly square, so a stitched design will seem slightly taller and narrower than the chart.

Burlap fabric can easily be counted and stitched over as you would on a traditional counted-thread fabric.

Threads for stitching

Most types of thread available for embroidery can be used for counted cross-stitch projects.

Six-ply cotton embroidery floss is available in the widest range of colors, including variegated colors. Six-ply floss is made to be separated easily into single or multiple plies for stitching. Instructions with each project in this book will tell you how many plies to use. A greater number of plies will result in a rich or heavy embroidered piece, few plies create a lightweight or fragile texture.

Rayon and silk floss is very similar in weight to cotton floss, but stitches have greater sheen. Either thread can be interchanged with cotton floss, one ply for one ply, but because they have a "slicker" texture, they are slightly more difficult to use.

Pearl cotton is available in four sizes: #3, #5, #8, and #12. (#3 is thick; #12 is thin.) It has an obvious twist and a high sheen.

Flower thread is a 100% cotton, matte-finish thread. A single strand of flower thread can be substituted for two plies of cotton floss.

Overdyed threads are being introduced on the market every day. Most of them have an irregularly variegated "one-of-a kind" appearance. Cotton floss, silk floss, flower thread, and pearl cotton weight threads are available in this form. All of them produce a soft shaded appearance without changing thread colors.

Specialty threads can add a distinctive look to cross-stitch They range in weight from hair-fine blending filament, usually used with floss, to $1/8$-inch-wide ribbon. They include numerous metallic threads, richly colored and textured threads, and fun-to-stitch, glow-in-the-dark threads.

Wool yarn, usually used for needlepoint or crewel embroidery, can be used for cross-stitch. Use one or two plies of three-ply Persian yarn. It is best to select evenweave fabrics with fewer threads per inch when working cross-stitches in wool yarn.

Ribbon in silk, rayon, and polyester becomes an interesting texture for cross-stitching, especially in combination with flower-shaped stitches. Look for straight-grain and bias-cut ribbons in solid and variegated colors and in widths from $1/16$ to $1 1/2$ inches.

Types of needles

Blunt-pointed needles are best for working on most cross-stitch fabrics because they slide through holes and between threads without splitting or snagging the fibers. A large-eyed needle accommodates the bulk of embroidery threads. Many companies sell such needles labeled "cross-stitch," but they are identical to tapestry needles, blunt tipped and large eyed. The chart, *above*, will guide you to the right size needle for most common fabrics.

One exception to blunt-tip needle rule is waste canvas; use sharp embroidery needles to poke through fabric.

Working with seed beads requires a very fine needle to slide through holes. Either a #8 quilting needle which is short with a tiny eye or a long beading needle with its longer eye are readily available. Some shops carry short beading needles with a long eye.

Fabric	Tapestry Needle size	Number of plies
11-count	24	Three
14-count	24-26	Two
18-count	26	Two
22-count	26	One

CROSS-STITCH TIPS

Preparing fabric

The edges of cross-stitch fabric take a lot of abrasion while a project is being stitched. There are many ways to keep fabric from fraying while you stitch.

The easiest and most widely available method is to bind the edges with masking tape. Because tape leaves a residue that's almost impossible to remove, it should be trimmed away after stitching is completed. All projects in this book that include tape in the instructions were planned with a large margin around the stitched fabric so tape can be trimmed away.

There are some projects where you should avoid tape. If a project does not have ample margins to trim away tape, use one of the techniques listed in the next paragraph.

If you have a sewing machine readily available, zigzag stitching, serging or narrow hemming are both neat and effective. Hand overcasting also works well, but is more time consuming.

Garments, table linens, towels, and other projects that will be washed on a regular basis when they are finished, should be washed before stitching to avoid shrinkage later. Wash the fabric in the same manner you will wash the finished project.

Preparing floss

Most cotton embroidery floss is color-fast and won't fade. A few bright colors, notably reds and greens, contain excess dye that could bleed onto fabrics if dampened. To remove the excess dye before stitching, gently slip off paper bands from floss and rinse each color in cool water until the water rinses clear. Then place floss on white paper toweling to dry. If there is any color on toweling when floss is dried, repeat the process. When completely dry, slip paper bands back on floss.

Centering the design

Most projects in this book instruct you to begin stitching at the center of the chart and fabric. To find the center of the chart, follow the horizontal and vertical arrows on the chart to the point where they intersect.

To find the center of the fabric, fold fabric in half horizontally, and baste along the fold. Fold fabric in half vertically and baste along fold. The point where basting intersects is the center of the fabric. Some stitchers like to add some additional lines of basting every ten or twenty rows as a stitching guide.

Cleaning your work

You may want to wash your needlecraft pieces before framing. The natural oils from your hands eventually will discolor the stitchery so it's a good idea to remove those oils before mounting and framing. Wash your piece by hand in cool water using mild detergent. Rinse several times, until the water is clear.

Do not wring or squeeze the needlecraft piece to get the water out. Hold the piece over the sink until dripping slows, then place flat on a clean terrycloth towel and roll tightly. Unroll the stitchery and lay flat to dry.

Pressing finished work

Carefully press the fabric from the back before framing or finishing. If the piece has lots of surface texture stitches, place it on a terrycloth towel or other padded surface to press.

Framing your design

Use determines how cross-stitch pieces should be mounted and framed. Needlework shops, professional framers, and craft stores offer many options for both.

For most purposes, omit the glass when framing your cross-stitch. Moisture can build up between the glass and the stitchery and sunlight is intensified by the glass. Both can cause damage to the fabric. If you must use glass, be sure to mat the piece so that the stitchery does not touch the glass.

INDEX

SOURCES/ SUPPLIERS

Many of the materials and items used in this book are available at craft and needlework stores. For more information, write the manufacturers below.

Chapter 1

Santa On His Way, page 7: Rayon floss—Susan Bates, Division of Coats & Clark.
Santa Mini-Banners, page 8: Trim—Heritage Trimming, Parade Hill Rd., Barnstead, NH 03218, 603/435-6795; Delta Ceramcoat paints—Delta Technical Coatings, Inc., 800/423-4135, Customer Service; dowel ends—Lara's Crafts, Box 14567, Ft. Worth, TX 76117.
St. Nick Stockings, page 9: Klostern fabric—Wichelt Imports, Inc. R.R. 1, Stoddard, WI 54658; Heatherfield fabric—Wichelt Imports, Inc.; red trim—Hollywood Trims, 42005 Cook St., Suite 106, Palm Desert, CA 92260; gold jingle bell—Darice, Inc., 21160 Drake Rd., Strongville, OH 44136; 1-inch gold tassels—Hollywood Trims.

Chapter 2

Peppermint Diamonds Jewelry, page 30: Perforated plastic—Darice, Inc.
Black and Gold Jewelry, page 30: Perforated plastic—Darice, Inc.
Celestial Button Covers, page 31: Perforated plastic—Darice, Inc.; beads—Mill Hill Seed Beads, 800/447-1332.

Chapter 3

Santa Cardholder, page 43: Novelty thread—Madeira Marketing Ltd., 385 W. Second Avenue, Eugene, OR 97401.
Noel Bell Pull, page 44: Decorative bell pull holder—Stitch & Frame, 6000 Douglas, Des Moines, IA 50322; banding—Wichelt Imports, Inc.

Chapter 4

Beaded Bag and Belt Buckle, page 67: Beads—Gick Crafts, 9 Studebaker Drive, Irvine, CA 92718.
Holly Towel and Napkin, page 68: Towel and napkin—Charles Craft, P.O. Box 1049, Laurinberg, NC 28353, 800/277-0980.
Sleigh Party Favor, page 69: Perforated plastic—Darice, Inc.; Ribbonfloss—Rhode Island Textile Company, P.O. Box 999, Pawtucket, RI 02862-0999.
Snowman Place Cards, page 69: Perforated paper—Yarn Tree, 117 Alexander St., P.O. Box 724, Ames, IA 50010, 800/247-3952; card stock—The Art Store, 600 Martin Luther King Jr. Parkway, Des Moines, IA 50312.

Chapter 5

Little Angel Stocking, page 83: Snowflake Charms—JHB International, Inc., 1955 S. Quince St., Denver, CO 80231; press-on fleece—Dritz Corp, P.O. Box 5028, Spartansburg, SC 29304; jingle bells—Darice, Inc.; ribbon—C.M. Offray & Sons, Inc.,

Route 24, Box 601, Chester, NJ 07930, 908/879-4700.
Heavenly Choir Sampler, page 85: Beads—Mill Hill.
Sweetness and Lace Angel, page 85: Perforated plastic—Darice, Inc.

Chapter 6

Paper Dolls, page 94: Perforated paper—Yarn Tree.
Circus Pull Toys, page 95: Perforated plastic—Darice, Inc.; round buttons—Streamline Industries Inc., 845 Stewart Ave., Garden City, NY 11530; sun, heart, and star buttons—JHB International, Inc.; colored wood beads—Westrim Crafts, Western Trimming Corp., Chatsworth, CA 91311; white tiny buttons—Streamline Industries Inc.
Candyland Checkers, pages 96–97: wooden box—Sudberry House, Box 895, Old Lyme, CT 06371; perforated plastic—Darice, Inc.

Chapter 7

Hardanger Christmas Trees Ornament, page 110: Watercolor Floss—The Caron Collection, 67 Poland St., Bridgeport, CT 06605, 203/333-0325.

FABRICS

Charles Craft, P.O. Box 1049, Laurinberg, NC 28353, 800/277-0980; Wichelt, Imports, Inc., R.R. 1, Stoddard, WI 54658; Zweigart, 2 Riverview Dr., Somerset, NJ 08873-1139, 908/271-1949.

THREADS

Anchor, Consumer Service Dept., P.O. Box 27067, Greenville, SC 29616; DMC, Port Kearney Bldg. 10, South Kearney, NJ 07032-0650; Kreinik Manufacturing, 800/537-2166.

Framing: Dot's Frame Shop, 4223 Fleur Dr., Des Moines, IA 50321.